ADDITIONAL PR
SACRED SIGNS & ⌣ ⌐ ⱭⱭⱯ

"Sherrie Dillard guides you to interpret the many messages of life in practical and meaningful ways … This book shows you the way to your intuitive power."

—Erin Byron, MA, author of *Yoga for the Creative Soul*
and *Yoga Therapy for Stress & Anxiety*

"*Sacred Signs & Symbols* offers profound knowledge as well as inspiring stories and techniques to help us pay attention to the intuitive input and signposts along the path of life."

—Diana Henderson, ascension artist, intuitive,
Reiki master teacher, and author of *Grandfather Poplar*
and the upcoming nonfiction book, *Kindred of the Crystal Kingdom*

Sacred Signs
& Symbols

ABOUT THE AUTHOR

Sherrie had been a professional psychic, medium, and medical intuitive for over thirty years. She has taught intuitive development at Duke University and teaches intuitive and spiritual development and spiritual healing workshops and classes nationally and internationally. She lives in Raleigh, NC. Visit her website at www.sherriedillard.com.

SHERRIE DILLARD

AWAKEN TO THE MESSAGES & SYNCHRONICITIES
THAT SURROUND YOU

Sacred SIGNS
& SYMBOLS

Llewellyn Publications
Woodbury, Minnesota

FIRST EDITION
First Printing, 2017

Cover design: Ellen Lawson
Editing: Patti Frazee

Llewellyn Publications is a registered trademark of Llewellyn Worldwide Ltd.

Library of Congress Cataloging-in-Publication Data
Names: Dillard, Sherrie, author.
Title: Sacred signs and symbols : awaken to the messages & synchronicities
    that surround you / Sherrie Dillard.
Description: First edition. | Woodbury : Llewellyn Worldwide, Ltd, 2017. |
    Includes bibliographical references and index.
Identifiers: LCCN 2017012905 (print) | LCCN 2017016962 (ebook) | ISBN
    9780738752143 (ebook) | ISBN 9780738749686 (alk. paper)
Subjects: LCSH: Parapsychology—Miscellanea. | Occultism—Miscellanea. |
    Signs and symbols--Miscellanea. | Symbolism—Miscellanea.
Classification: LCC BF1040 (ebook) | LCC BF1040 .D555 2017 (print) | DDC
    133.3—dc23
LC record available at https://lccn.loc.gov/2017012905

Llewellyn Worldwide Ltd. does not participate in, endorse, or have any authority or responsibility concerning private business transactions between our authors and the public.
    All mail addressed to the author is forwarded but the publisher cannot, unless specifically instructed by the author, give out an address or phone number.
    Any Internet references contained in this work are current at publication time, but the publisher cannot guarantee that a specific location will continue to be maintained. Please refer to the publisher's website for links to authors' websites and other sources.

Llewellyn Publications
A Division of Llewellyn Worldwide Ltd.
2143 Wooddale Drive
Woodbury, MN 55125-2989
www.llewellyn.com

Printed in the United States of America

Other Books by Sherrie Dillard

Discover Your Psychic Type

Love and Intuition

You Are a Medium

Develop Your Medical Intuition

Discover Your Authentic Self

Forthcoming Books by Sherrie Dillard

You Are Psychic

Dedicated to my sister, Dawn Marie, and grandson, Henry William. Guiding sparks of love and light. Although your time among us was brief, your message endures and continues to transform.

———

Thank you to the wonderful people at Llewellyn for keeping the door to new ideas, truths, and realities open for so many years and for so many of us here in the physical and spiritual worlds.

Special thank you to the creative and kind Angela Wix—you are always the best. Kathy Schneider for keeping the wheels turning. Patti Frazee for her hawklike vision. Kat Sanborn for spreading the news and all those who contributed their time and energy to getting this book out into the world.

Vast gratitude to the birds, the trees, and especially the nature deities who showed up and insisted that I pay attention to the signs and guided the development of this book. You all made it so much fun!

Contents

YOU ARE THE CENTER OF THE ORACLE

You are standing in the center of a very chatty universe that is ready to engage. Everything you encounter is a part of you and you are part of it. Even though you may at times feel separate and unknown in a vast and impersonal world, you are never as alone as you may think. No matter where you are and what you are doing, you are being guided and led. A loving and wise divine spiritual power and presence watches over and cares for you. One of the ways the spiritual realm seeks to guide, comfort, and inspire you is by sending you signs, messages, and synchronicities.

Do you ever find coins or feathers on your path and wonder if this is a message from someone or something? Does the same species of bird suspiciously come to your window a little too often for it to be simply a chance encounter? Do you wake at the same time night after night, then glance at the clock at this same time during the day? When facing a difficult choice, decision, or during a personal crisis, have you ever asked for a sign or message to guide and lead you? If any of these are true for you, you are not alone.

Since the beginning of time we have looked to an invisible presence and power to guide and comfort us through signs and messages. When you notice signs, you are pulled into the deeper mystery of life where you become aware that you are seen, known, and being guided.

USING SIGNS FOR GUIDANCE

From a young age I have seen, felt, and communicated with spirit beings such as angels, people who have passed over to the other side, spirit guides, and ascended masters. They have communicated to me through feelings of love and comfort. I have heard their wise counsel through an inner voice and they have led me through signs and synchronicities. It is always a special treat to encounter one of their gifts. A feather, a synchroncity that seems almost impossible to be a coincidence, a seashell, or a visit from an owl are a few of the ways they get my attention.

I enjoy communicating with the sprit realm so much that I have made a professional career out of it. During my almost thirty years of being a professional intuitive and medium, I have frequently been asked what intuitive techniques I most often use to tune in to my personal concerns and questions. People are usually surprised when I tell them that I routinely ask for and look to signs and messages for guidance and to validate my intuitive impressions.

If you have ever tried to access intuitive guidance when you needed to make an important decision or in the midst of a personal crisis, you may have been frustrated by the result. Although we often look to our intuition to provide wise and timely insight, achieving the calm and receptive state that is needed to receive clear intuitive guidance can be difficult. Unfortunately, it often seems that when we most need the assuring voice of our intuition, our stress levels make it almost impossible to become quiet and meditative enough to receive inner guidance. The same is true when a loved one on the other side reaches out to connect with us. Our grief over their passing and the many other intense emotions that we often feel can create an energetic static that gets in the way of tuning in to their presence. Our intuitive awareness can seem to be blocked or absent and it becomes all too easy to mistake our desires, wishes, and hopes as intuitive information or to discount our intuitive impressions altogether.

If you find yourself pressed for answers, overthinking, and becoming consumed with trying to figure out possibilities, options, choices, and the best course to take, there is another option. The divine spirit realm knows all too well the difficulties that you encounter and has devised creative ways to break through the chattering, thinking mind and anxious emotions. Your prayers and requests for spiritual help and intervention are heard and answered. However, the divine response may not come in the way that you expect or desire. To become aware of the guidance that you are seeking, it is necessary to let go of the way that you want the answer to come to you and be open and receptive to the many ways spirit communicates.

Signs, messages, and synchronicities are messages from above. Through them the spirit realm sends their wise and loving council in a dependable and accessible way. When you observe and notice signs and messages, you come into the here and now. Instead of worrying, obsessing, or feeling lonely, renewed hope and heart-centered awareness is awakened.

THE POWER OF SIGNS

Over the years I have looked to signs and messages for guidance on minor issues as well as life-changing decisions. I rarely make an important decision without some form of sign confirmation. As you can imagine, over the years I have encountered many signs. Some have foretold of upcoming positive events, while others have helped me make good choices or warned me to be cautious or careful. Some have given me direction on day-to-day issues, while others have guided me in soul growth and purpose and graced me with transformative healing.

Sacred signs, messages, and synchronicities can alleviate our worries and alert us to the presence of powerful spiritual forces. Just recently, I encountered this kind of healing sign. Soon after my four-year-old granddaughter was diagnosed with an autoimmune illness, she was admitted to the hospital and underwent emergency surgery. Two weeks later she was released from the hospital, only to be readmitted a few days later when an ultrasound discovered a sack of fluid in her abdomen. The doctors feared that her intestinal surgery was leaking or that there was some kind of infection.

The day before she went back into the hospital a client gave me a pair of socks with the woven image of Guadalupe on the side. She told me that she was shopping before our session, and when she saw the socks, she felt that she had to buy them for me. I knew that this was a sign. I had been praying to the Divine Mother for healing for my granddaughter. When I saw the socks, I knew in my heart that she would be okay.

A day later my granddaughter, still in the intensive care unit, underwent a procedure to drain the fluid from her abdomen. However, the doctor and his team did not find any. Perplexed, they performed a CT scan in an attempt to discover where the sack of fluid was hiding. It could not be located and after a thorough search they realized that it was no longer there. The fluid had disappeared, the autoimmune outbreaks subsided, and she has not had a reoccurrence of the illness since.

CREATING THE ORACLE

Along with looking to signs for guidance, from a young age I have also consulted a variety of different oracle systems. I have sought advice from the runes, studied the tarot cards, and threw coins to create hexagrams from the I Ching, or the Book of Changes. A couple of years ago, I began to get a message to develop an oracle system. Yet, I was not sure what type of oracle guidance system to create. Intent of figuring this out I asked for a sign or message to help point me in the right direction. I soon experienced an outpouring of them. I received so many signs I knew I was on the right track, but I was still not sure how to proceed. Then one afternoon while walking my dog, I found a large hawk feather close to the steps of a church. When I saw it, I intuitively knew that finding this beautiful feather near a church in a busy urban area was an important sign. As I picked the feather up a message shot through me like a bolt of lightning. I became instantly and intuitively aware that the signs I had been receiving were guiding me to create a sign oracle. It made perfect sense.

In my work as a psychic and medium, I am always amazed by the unique and clever ways that my clients' angels, loved ones on the other side, spirit guides, and other spirit beings attempt to get their attention and extend help and love. They want us to know they are with us and that guidance, insight, and healing is always close. Unfortunately, when we are stressed or rushing about, we often miss many of the guiding signs sent our way. When we do notice them, we may not always be able to understand and interpret their meaning.

The Living Oracle was created with these things in mind. It provides you with a framework through which you can better notice and invoke sacred signs, messages, and synchronicities, and interpret their guidance and meaning.

How to Use this Book

Like many people, you may at times wonder if you are being given a sign or message. Even when you see, hear, notice, and encounter signs, messages, and synchronicities, you may find yourself wanting to believe in them but quickly talking yourself out of it. When you do recognize a sign, you may wonder and question who is sending it to you and why. Signs, messages, and synchronicities may appear to be random, as they often come to us in ways that bypasses the logical and rational. We do not always notice them and when we do, we all too often dismiss them and doubt their validity.

If you find yourself questioning if you have received a sign, or if you are confused as to who or what may have sent it your way, you are not alone. Sacred signs and messages break through time and space and present us with a touch of the heavens. Because they do not always fit within the parameters of what we believe to be possible, we often miss important connections and guidance.

No matter where you are and what you are doing, signs and messages are present, even if you do not notice them. The spiritual force that generates them is reliable, loving, and intelligent, and always in operation. The divine presence is everywhere and in all things. If you are on the edge of believing and trusting the notion that there is a spiritual force and power that can offer you guidance and healing, let me give you a little nudge. Instead of dismissing and ignoring the grace and gifts being sent your way, you can learn how to better accept, trust, and embrace them.

The journey begins in the first section where you will learn how to better recognize the telltale characteristics of signs and messages and better decipher who or what may be sending them to your way.

Invoking

Many sacred signs, messages, and synchronicities come to us uninvited. During times of confusion or stress, when we need to make a decision, or even when all is well, we may suddenly become aware that the butterfly that just landed on our windowsill or the cloud overhead that is shaped like a heart may be a message. When we notice and trust that we are being guided, the sudden appearance of a sign can be a welcome relief. They remind us that we are not alone. They can fill us with love, provide us with much-needed direction, and give us the assurance that our concerns and worries are being worked out for the highest good.

You can live in continuous connection and communion with a higher presence and power. Signs and messages are a form of communication that is available at all times and under any circumstances. Anyone can practice and participate in noticing signs and messages. You do not have to be especially gifted or a confident intuitive to benefit from unspoken and spiritual guidance.

Even though signs often come to us without our request, you can invoke them when you most need guidance, comfort, and direction. When you request sacred signs and messages for guidance or a specific question or issue, they become an oracle. The Living Oracle is an organic and natural phenomenon that empowers you to invoke and interpret the signs and messages that the divine sends your way. It is a bridge of communication between you and the divine. This timeless connection between the physical and spiritual realms has always existed and you can reclaim your natural ability to receive guidance when you most need it.

With the Living Oracle you can ask for a sign or message for any concern or condition. There is no area of your life that is too mundane or unimportant. Signs speak to our relationships, career, and life purpose. They guide us in our everyday decisions and choices, offer spiritual guidance, and connect us to our loved ones on the other side and our angels.

The Living Oracle begins with noticing signs for a specific amount of time within a defined area. This is called casting the oracle. In the second section you learn a few different ways to cast a sign oracle. Inspired by ancient practices, oracles can be cast while taking a walk, sitting on a park bench, or by simply looking out your window and observing signs for a specific amount of time. The Living Oracle provides insight into your current circumstances and questions and reveals what you most need to become aware of at the time of the casting.

The Language of Signs

Throughout history, oracle systems have looked to nature and naturally occurring phenomena, such as the changing skies, the flight patterns of birds, markings on sticks and stones, and the sightings of animals to provide us with guidance and direction. Although many ancient oracle systems make use of the symbology of nature and the natural world, signs and messages emerge in everyday conditions and through everyday objects and situations. The advancement of technology and contemporary society has allowed new and creative signs and messages to develop and take shape. Even though some signs and messages are similar in appearance and meaning to those that occurred centuries ago, they also take form and are expressed through everyday conditions, objects, and situations.

The Living Oracle was designed as a way to better notice and interpret the common signs that often occur in more urban areas such as towns, cities, and residential areas and neighborhoods. It is in highly populated areas that signs, messages, and synchronicities are often missed or ignored.

The purpose and meaning of present-day signs and messages and centuries old, naturally occurring ones might not always be obvious. Signs and messages communicate through symbolic and metaphoric language. Some signs utilize time-honored universal symbols, while others are expressed in a more personal and individual way.

Along with listening within to your intuition and gut knowing and relying on your personal interpretation of signs and messages, there is an extensive glossary in the last section of the book to assist you in understanding the meaning within the signs that you are likely to encounter. Through the direction of wise, knowledgeable, and sometimes funny spirit beings, I have been provided with insight into the interpretation of many natural and contemporary and urban signs. This sign glossary will empower you to better decipher and successfully utilize in your everyday concerns and conditions the meaning, guidance, and direction encoded within most of the signs that you encounter.

Sacred Relationship

As much as sacred signs, messages, and synchronicities guide, comfort, and empower us to make wise decisions and choices, they are also an invitation into a true and lasting relationship with a divine, loving, and wise spiritual power. When you accept this invitation the world of random and meaningless events and circumstances begins to fall away. In its place a holy presence walks with you. Life begins to make sense as the doors to a transcendent adventure swing open. New awareness replaces confusion and connection when a loving and wise higher power fills the void of emptiness. All of life becomes a Living Oracle where you are supported, loved, and cared for.

PART 1

UNDERSTANDING THE SIGNS THAT SURROUND YOU

Throughout your day there are likely numerous signs and messages that appear and seek to guide and comfort you. Some you may notice, but most you likely do not. This first section provides you with insight to the many different types of sacred signs and messages and who may be sending them to you and why.

CHAPTER 1

A VERY BRIEF HISTORY OF SIGNS

Observing signs and omens and discerning guidance from them is an innate and primal knowledge that we all share. In virtually every civilization in history, connection between external phenomena and human consciousness was observed, honored, and revered. We had a shared perception of the world as dreamlike. Nature, objects, and the skies spoke to us and conveyed hidden and prophetic guidance. Our present experience of feeling separate from one another and our spiritual source and living in a meaningless world is far removed from the depth and richness that early humans experienced.

In ancient societies where signs and messages were revered, there was a code of communication that was inherent and present within all of life. It held the key to the unknown and led us in making individual and collective choices. Through our attentiveness to sacred signs and messages, we were led to a deeper understanding and awareness of our place in the cosmos. We listened when we encountered something that spoke to us. When we needed to make a decision or to know whether or not to proceed with a new venture, we looked to the world around us for guidance and direction. Our intuition was a normal and natural sense that we trusted to help us discern and understand the inherent meaning within the signs that we encountered. In this way our interconnectedness to spiritual forces was celebrated.

ASSIGNING MEANING TO SIGNS

Early humans became aware of the symbolic meaning within natural objects, animals, birds, and other phenomena by studying and becoming aware of the conditions and changes that were simultaneously occurring in the human realm at the time that signs were observed. This is called synchronicty, or meaningful coincidences. By becoming aware of natural events and the corresponding and related conditions, changes, or patterns in human affairs, meaning and messages were attributed to specific phenomena. In present time we often make these same kind of connections.

For instance, when I was young, I walked to elementary school with my older sister by way of a shortcut that took us through the woods and over a small wooden footbridge. One morning as I approached this bridge, I noticed a large black crow sitting on it. I immediately knew that his presence had meaning. I felt a little light-headed as he stood still, looking at me. I wanted to run away but instead opted to walk around the bridge and jump over the small stream. Although I had a sense that the crow had a message for me, I had no idea what it was.

Later that evening during dinner, my mother abruptly and almost nonchalantly told me and my three siblings that my father would no longer be living with us. There was no discussion. We all just sat in stunned and quiet despair. Filled with sadness, I finished eating and went out to the backyard. There sitting on our fence, against the setting sun, was a crow. I did not know for sure if it was the same crow I had encountered that morning, but I wanted to believe that it was. It seemed to intensely stare at me and a shiver of energy ran up my spine. I both wanted to confide and share my grief with it and shoo it away. I did neither. I just looked at it and felt an inner knowing that everything was going to be okay. I wanted to believe that something or someone was watching over me and had sent the crow to let me know that I was not alone. As darkness descended the crow eventually left and I went back in the house, feeling a surprising sense of comfort.

Over the years I have developed an understanding of the symbolic language of signs and messages. They have become a natural source of guidance and enlightened understanding that I never regret listening to and acting on.

SIGNS THROUGHOUT HISTORY

Across the globe and in many different cultures, nature, natural phenomena, and objects were believed to embody messages and signs and the presence of wise and loving spiritual forces. For instance, like many other early cultures, ancient Romans believed that objects and all living beings possessed spiritual and magical properties. The trees, mountains, caves, lakes, and animals were believed to embody spirits. The weather, lightning in particular, water, and especially stones that bordered property were bearers of important messages. In Celtic and Norse mythology animals, and in particular birds, were powerful messengers. The Norse god Odin is sometimes referred to as the raven god. The visitation or sighting of a raven could be either an auspicious sign or bad omen depending on the current conditions and circumstances. In ancient China and most of Asia, crickets were thought of as watchdogs. When they stopped chirping, danger was near. Dew on the ground was considered auspicious and frogs were an important omen that brought the promise of abundance, prosperity, love, friendship, and fertility.

At the beginning of new ventures such as births, planting seasons, going to war, or making a personal or a collective decision, signs and omens in most cultures were particularly sought and had the most power. For instance, in ancient northern Europe a woman would feel a heightened sense of joy and promise when wanting to conceive a child if she discovered a bird's nest with eggs. In many regions ancient sailors who had spent months at sea knew that land was near when dolphins came close to their ship.

In critical moments when decisions needed to be made or the future foretold, omens and signs had the power to change the course of history. For instance, in ancient Rome, a planned attack would go forward if an important official spotted a flowering palm, a sign that guaranteed success in battle. Changes in the skies were especially important as they were viewed as direct messages from the gods. For instance, in many cultures solar eclipses influenced warring opponents to make peace and motivated others to declare war and invade rival empires. Comets had a similar effect. According to legend, when Genghis Khan observed Halley's Comet in 1222, he took it as a sign to move his troops westward into the heart of Europe.

DIVINATION SYSTEMS

In ancient times, observing signs and omens became an essential and common method to discern the will of spiritual forces and make decisions and choices. Because of their effectiveness and reliability, ancient people took the evolutionary step and began to invent divination systems to invoke and utilize signs and omens.

One of the oldest-known divination systems is the Chinese I Ching, or Book of Changes. It is based on the recurrence of six numbers or lines, which create the possibility of sixty-four hexagrams. Originally bones or yarrow sticks were used to cast a hexagram. Three coins are now more commonly used. Each hexagram explains and describes natural forces and conditions and the corresponding human challenge or change that it represents. Modern scholars believe that the original text was assembled sometime around 1000 BC. Confucius is said to be the I Ching's greatest patron. He devoted much of his life to contemplating the hexagrams and adding interpretation and commentaries to the original text.

Thousands of miles away in northern Europe, markings on rocks and sticks and branches were being observed as a potent source of guidance and wisdom. Within these natural configurations, the Germanic/Norse perceived the spirit of the gods and discerned their advice on human affairs. From this awareness they created the runes, a series of twenty-four stones, tiles, or wooden blocks marked with a symbol or letter that served as both an alphabet and a divination system. The earliest runic inscriptions date from around 150 AD.

The tarot cards are another divination system that has influenced and guided people in all cultures across the globe. The first documented tarot cards were created between 1430 and 1450 in northern Italy, but many researchers believe their roots trace back to ancient

Egypt and the Kabbalah. There is no official tarot card deck. Many modern decks contain images and symbols of ancient, naturally occurring patterns, signs, and archetypes. From the early tarot decks, divination cards of all types, spiritual paths, and philosophies have emerged. Divination cards are likely the most common contemporary oracle method for invoking guidance and direction.

These and other well-utilized divination systems have withstood the test of time. Their popularity and longevity is a testament to the wisdom, guidance, and direction that they have provided to people throughout centuries of change and evolution. These systems and many other similar ones have their basis in the observation of signs and omens and the intuitive insight of early civilizations.

SCIENTIFIC AND NOT-SO-SCIENTIFIC DISCOVERIES

After thousands of years of relying on the world around us for intuitive and symbolic guidance and awareness, a gradual shift began to take place. Trust and faith in physical proof and measurable evidence as a standard for discerning fact and truth began to gain momentum.

Initiated in ancient Greece, the practice of seeking knowledge through focusing on physical science and experimentation began to spread. By the seventeenth century, the primary means of determining reality through scientific inquiry reached a pinnacle of development in Europe.

Over time the awareness and trust in signs and omens to provide guidance and foretell the future was, for the most part, sidelined by contemporary cultures as superstitious and irrational. However, a few pioneers in the Western world challenged this trend and became aware of and discerned the inherent power and symbolic potential within naturally occurring signs and messages. Most prominent among them is psychiatrist Carl Jung, who studied the importance of unscientific phenomena and brought this awareness into contemporary focus. He was the first scientist to observe and discuss meaningful coincidences, which he termed synchronicity. It was in his psychiatric practice while listening to the dreams of his patients that he first became aware of this phenomenon. Jung noticed that the dream symbols discussed by his patients often appeared in their life as unexpected coincidences. When this synchronicity occurred, healing often spontaneously came about and therapy was more successful.

One of the early defining experiences that led to Jung's interest in synchronicities involved a patient's dream of a scarabaeid beetle. His patient, who did not seem to be making progress in therapy, recounted to Jung a dream she had where someone gave her a golden scarab. At the same time that she was recounting this dream, Jung heard a tapping on the window. When he opened it, a gold-green scarabaeid beetle, similar to the one described in the dream, flew into the room. Catching the beetle in his hand, Jung handed it to his patient. Just as the dream foretold.

The shock and surprise of the sudden appearance of the beetle had a transformative effect on the woman. Jung recounted that her resistance diminished and from that point on she made swift progress in healing.

COMING FULL CIRCLE

Although the phenomenon of synchronicity was first scientifically investigated by Carl Jung, new advancements in science have opened doors to a better understanding of how energy responds and is influenced by our thoughts and intent. The study of physics, especially quantum physics, has demonstrated the unified effect of energy. Simply stated, this scientific observation demonstrates that every single particle in the universe has a gravitational effect upon every other particle, no matter how far away the particles are separated. The unified effect can, in part, help to explain the science behind synchronicities, signs, and messages. What we think and feel, along with our intent, exerts an influence on our environment.

Exciting advancements like these are moving us closer to understanding the science behind the manifestation of signs and messages. However, there are still forces and realities that, as of yet, cannot be measured in a laboratory. The presence of divine life force energy is present in all things and it influences our environment and what we experience. What we perceive in our everyday life unfolds from the deeper layers of human consciousness, thought, and belief, and from the unseen energy of the universe.

Instead of overthinking, worrying, and feeling anxious, trust in the benevolence of a meaningful universe that offers you clarity and direction. Let the world speak to you and reveal its guiding presence. Let it come alive and transform random and seemingly insignificant events into a treasure trove of insight and meaning.

CHAPTER 2

HOW TO SPOT A SIGN

Sacred signs, messages, and synchronicities appear in a multitude of expressions and forms. Some are easier to notice and understand than others. Quite often we may sense or feel that we have encountered a sign, but then all too often dismiss it for lack of concrete evidence. Although signs and messages speak to our intuitive nature and frequently bypass logic and reasoning, they tend to have telltale characteristics and attributes that can alert you to their presence. Adopt an open-minded and curious attitude and they will begin to come to life all around you.

SYMBOLOGY

Sacred signs, messages, and synchronicities use the unique language of metaphor and symbology to convey guidance and direction. When you perceive all that you encounter and experience through a symbolic lens, even the most inert and mundane object or event can transform itself into a guiding oracle.

Since the beginning of time, we have used symbolic language to express ideas, feelings, thoughts, beliefs, and spiritual awareness. Egyptian hieroglyphics, the Mayan calendar, and the runes are a few of the early symbolic systems that were developed to communicate and express meaningful information. Mysteries and complex ideas that are difficult to explain and comprehend are often best understood through symbology.

As an example, one of the most popular symbolic systems is astrology. Astrologically, the sun represents the sign of Leo and the individual self. The moon represents the sign of Cancer and the intuitive, emotional nature. In Chinese astrology, each year is represented by an animal. Each of these creatures represents innate characteristics and personality traits of the individuals born in that year. The year characterized by the animal also foretells the positive and negative potential of the year. For instance, someone born under the year of the rabbit is said to be agreeable, noble, and not aggressive. The year of the horse is said to be a good year to start new projects and take relationships to a higher level. Planets are also associated with certain characteristics and embody specific energetic attributes. Venus is the planet of love, beauty, and harmony while Saturn represents limitation, structure, and time.

We regularly use symbols to convey specific attributes and represent qualities and ideals. For instance, athletic teams use symbols to establish the characteristics that they would like to embody and project. For example, the Wild Cats, Bears, Giants, Hawks, Pirates, and Hurricanes are a few of the symbols professional sports teams use to represent their brand. Some symbols are so common we don't give them a second thought. Common symbolic associations include such things as hearts and love, four-leaf clovers and luck, and the color red with stop and green with go.

Signs and messages communicate in a similar way. Everyday objects, activities, things, and natural occurrences can represent specific attributes and characteristics. Many of the signs you may encounter contain symbols that have globally understood and accepted meaning. For instance, water is symbolic of emotion and spiritual energy. A rainbow is symbolic of happiness and fulfillment.

There are also signs that are more personal in meaning. As an example, my friend Emma has always felt a connection with turtles. She felt that they were symbolic of slowing down, peace, and wisdom. When she came across a painting at an art fair of turtles lined up on a log, she had to have it.

Besides loving the painting, she felt that there was a message within it that she needed to pay attention to. Busy working two jobs, she knew that she needed to slow down and take time to pursue her creative passion. She had wanted to take a jewelry design class for some time. As she contemplated the message of the painting, she realized that it was a sign for her to work just one job and use the extra time to develop her creativity.

When you begin to develop an appreciation of the symbolic meaning contained within all things, it becomes easier to notice signs and understand their message.

Exercise to Strengthen Symbolic Awareness

All that you encounter during your day-to-day routines and activities can speak to you. Encoded within all form is the energy and wisdom of the formless. What you notice and experience is symbolic of your feelings, thoughts, desires, and beliefs. Not only does the world around you respond and express your energy, it also expresses your higher self and the divine presence.

When you notice and understand the symbolic meaning of things and activities, you can make enlightened choices and flow within the current of divine support. With a little practice you can develop symbolic vision, which will empower you to better decipher the meaning within signs and messages.

Try This

To begin, see with beginner's eyes, without judgment and preconceived ideas, as to what something is and is not.

Notice one object or thing in your immediate environment. What draws your attention and seems to have a message for you?

For instance, when I look around my room the first thing that draws my attention is a lamp.

What comes to mind in relation to the object that draws your attention? Freely associate other meanings and connections that the object my have.

Besides bringing light to the room and allowing me to see other objects and things. I realize that the lamp offers light, illuminates the darkness, and aids in seeing in more detail and depth.

Now ask yourself: is there a condition or situation in your life where you may need more clarity or to see something in more depth and detail?

> *For instance, what comes to mind for me is a family situation where I feel left out in the dark. I would like to better understand and have more clarity as to how my family members will work out their situation and if there is anything I can do to help them. Perhaps the message of the light is symbolic of my desire to have someone or something "turn on the light" and help me to perceive this situation more clearly and become aware of what my role may be in it.*

The more you practice perceiving everyday things and events symbolically, the more you will be able to discern and understand the signs that a loving and wise higher power is sending your way. There is no right or wrong answer, trust what feels right for you.

REPETITION

Signs and messages are repetitive. They tend to occur over and over until we acknowledge them and understand their meanings. If we do not notice a particular sign, another sign may appear in an attempt to better get our attention. Sometimes when we ignore or fail to perceive signs they gradually increase in intensity in an attempt to get our attention. When this happens the soft nudge of a gentle message can build momentum and become a disruptive event.

This is what Claire, a client of mine and a project manager at a technology firm, experienced. Although she felt in her heart that her purpose was to help other women develop business leadership skills and abilities, she did not act on it. Opportunities to become a certified business coach and requests from colleagues for guidance still came her way, but she ignored the synchronicity of these opportunities. She told herself when she was less busy, she would look into it.

One morning on her way to work, a hawk came swooping down close to her car only to turn around and again fly unusually close. She knew that this was a sign but didn't understand its meaning. Later that week she was called into her manager's office where she was told that the company was making broad layoffs. Her job, along with many others in her department, was being eliminated. She was given two weeks' notice.

After being let go, Claire went to her car to sit in the quiet and reflect on what had just happened. One by one she recalled the signs and synchronicities that had come her way in the past several months, all of which seemed to be directing her to a new line of work. She realized that someone or something was watching over and guiding her. With a sigh of relief, she felt that everything would work out. A soft feeling of peace and excitement for future possibilities moved through her when she committed to pursuing her heartfelt career desires.

TIMING

Be especially alert and observe patterns and synchronicities when you have a choice to make, when you are undecided about going forward with something, or when you begin a new relationship or undertaking.

Signs, messages, and synchronicities also often occur at the beginning of a project, enterprise, or life change. For instance, some Hindus in India may look for signs and omens when leaving the home to begin a new endeavor or go on a trip. When stepping out of the house, they may look and listen for auspicious signs such as hearing a pleasant conversation, seeing an umbrella, flowers, fans, or mirrors.

Naturally occurring signs tend to be more common during times of need, illness, loss, or during anniversaries or special occasions. They are also prevalent during times of celebrations, achievements, and milestones. Even if the world does not recognize a job well done, our personal growth, or accomplishing a personal goal, the spirit realm often does. Signs may also accompany and highlight an important event or connection.

For instance, Stella met Jake at her cousin's wedding. She was sipping champagne when the six-year-old flower girl came running toward her holding Jake's hand.

"It was almost like she was bringing me this wonderful gift," Stella said. "Our eyes met and I knew that he was special. There were two birds sitting on a tree limb not far from me, singing and chirping. I felt as if they were a sign that we were meant to meet."

PATTERNS

Signs and messages tend to come in repetitive patterns. In many of the ancient cultures that looked to the unseen for guidance and direction, the observance of patterns was a significant factor in identifying characteristics of signs and interpreting their message. In ancient China the cracks and markings on tortoise shells were considered signs and interpreted as an oracle. In many regions and cultures, including Roman, Greek, and Native American, the pattern that birds formed while flying overhead was used to foretell the outcome of upcoming conditions and events.

The observance of patterns is still helpful in identifying signs and interpreting their meaning and significance. For instance, glancing at a clock at 1:11 may not seem particularly significant, but glancing at a clock at 1:11 a few days in a row, or during the day and night, highlights its importance. Hearing the name of the same physician, therapist, or financial advisor from different sources within a few days signifies a sign. This is also true for finding feathers, pennies, or seeing butterflies. The more often a sign repeats itself or forms a pattern, the more likely it is an important sign or message. The meaning of a sign will also become more obvious when it forms a repetitive pattern that is connected to an event, condition, or desire.

INTUITION

Your intuition is a valuable tool through which you can better discern the presence of signs and messages. A natural and innate ability, there are four basic ways that we all naturally intuit. A mental intuitive intuits through thoughts or a sense of knowing, while an emotional intuitive intuits through emotions and feelings. A spiritual intuitive intuits energy information through the energy field or aura, and a physical intuitive receives energy information through the physical body or by holding objects or looking at photos.

Most people are a combination of these four intuitive types, with one or two that are more naturally developed. Understanding these four basic ways of intuiting will help you to become better aware of when you are receiving a sign as well as help you to understand and interpret its meaning.

A mental intuitive may become aware of a sign and its meaning through a spontaneous sense of knowing or through listening to their inner voice. Intuiting in this way differs from overthinking or analyzing, in that intuition is receptive and not active. You quickly know when you are in the presence of a sign and you do not have to try to understand it; you simply do.

A physical intuitive has the innate ability to tune in to messages from the natural world and can often intuit the energy contained within objects and photos. More than the other intuitive types, a physical intuitive may innately understand the meaning of signs that come through birds, animals, and other natural things and occurrences. In the presence of a sign, message, or synchronicity, a physical intuitive may experience tingling or shivers running up their spine or the hair of their arms may stand up.

For a spiritual intuitive, feelings of expansion and oneness with a greater power or presence often occurs when noticing a sign. Because they are more sensitive to the spirit realm, they may quickly intuit who or what has sent them a message or sign. A spiritual intuitive also has an easier time perceiving and understanding the symbolic language encoded within signs.

An emotional intuitive naturally receives the vibrations of love from the spirit realm. Compared to the other ways of intuiting, it may be easier for an emotional intuitive to open their heart and receive the healing and transformative energy within a sign. They may become alert to signs and synchronicities through spontaneous feelings of love and comfort. As they soak in the positive vibrations of the sign or message, its meaning unfolds and reveals itself.

Your intuition can empower you to go beyond superficial appearances and shallow understanding and perceive the deeper significance and meaning encoded within signs and messages.

TAKE THE LEAP

Perhaps the biggest obstacle to fully noticing and interpreting signs and messages is doubt and limited thinking. Even if you want to trust and believe that you have experienced a sign or message, there may be a voice within you that would like tangible proof. Unfortunately, signs do not usually come with concrete scientific evidence that fits neatly into the box of logic and reason.

When you encounter or experience what you believe to be a sign or message, you have the choice to take the leap and trust that there is a wise and benevolent higher power and presence that is guiding you, or to dismiss your experience as mere coincidence or magical thinking.

To make it easier to fully benefit from the inherent goodness within all of life, trust in a meaningful universe that knows and cares for you. Albert Einstein said: "If at first the idea is not absurd, then there is no hope for it." When you perceive a universe of unlimited possibilities, you can receive the full bounty of spiritual grace and presence.

As you let go of judgments and preconceived ideas of what is possible, you come into a more receptive state of awareness. Mindfulness is the ability to be present in the moment and to be aware of what is, with full acceptance of your thoughts, feelings, and sensations. Noticing and discerning signs and synchronicities requires a similar state of attentive, open, and nonjudgemental awareness. When we are busy rushing about and overthinking, it is easy to miss the signs and messages that are being sent our way. It is even more difficult to experience and embrace their guidance, comfort, and connection and message.

The ability to notice and gain insight from signs and messages churns deep in our collective unconscious. Open your heart and mind and fully trust. Doubt is focused in the material perspective. It is not able to penetrate beyond the boundaries of finite reasoning. Even when you doubt, signs and messages will still come your way. The spirit realm is constantly emanating its love and guidance. Yet, when you attempt to control what is happening by being overly skeptical, you shut the door to beneficial support and direction. A grateful and open heart and mind allows you to receive the healing and transformative power of a sign or synchronicity.

Chapter 3

The Messengers

Sacred signs, messages, and synchronicities challenge the assumption that the heavens and earth are separate and at a distance from one another. Wherever you are and whatever you are doing, spiritual guidance, love, comfort, and support are close by. There are many devoted spirit beings who are watching over you and doing their best to send you signs and messages.

Messages, signs, and synchronicities seem to come randomly and by chance, yet there is a guiding force of intelligence and love that places them on your path. They are the voice of the most holy within you and outside of you. Although we tend to feel alone at times, we never are. Consciousness and life is everywhere. Even though we cannot see or touch who and what may be close and by our side, spiritual help and influence is reliable and always present.

It is not always possible or necessary to know the origin of a sign, message, or synchronicity or who may have specifically sent it your way. However, we are still curious and would like to know who is close and guiding us.

The spirit realm has many messengers. Angels, archangels, ascended masters, spirit guides, loved ones on the other side, earth and nature spirits, and your higher self; all send signs to you and can make themselves known in very clever and heart-inspiring ways.

ANGELS

Angels are pure divine presence. Although they may appear in human form, they are not part of the human race. Instead they are timeless eternal divine beings who emanate the highest degree of love, compassion, and goodness. Since your birth you have had a guardian angel who has been watching over you and guiding you. They cannot interfere with your free will and decisions. Yet, they do their best to send you messages and signs of guidance, comfort, and support.

Many of the common signs that an angel uses to let you know of their presence are similar to the kind of signs loved ones on the other side often send. Butterflies, birds, rainbows, seashells, feathers—especially white ones—flowers, or the scent of flowers come by way of the angelic realm. Angels can play with the clouds, often forming unique shapes to get our attention, and may send us a warm, pleasantly scented breeze. Sometimes a high-pitched ringing in your ears or hearing a soft, inner melody signals the presence of an angel.

Yet, the strongest telltale sign of the presence of an angel may be the feeling of love, inspiration, joy, and the knowing that everything is going to be okay. In times of stress, pain, loneliness, and loss, they are particularly close. Angels, particularly archangels, often send messages via numbers. The most common of which are 1, 11, 2, 22, 7, or combinations of these. Numbers are energy portals. Your angel may influence you to look at clocks at a particular time or notice repeating numbers as a way to shift your awareness to a higher vibration. Although we are often confused and not aware of the meaning behind the frequent observance of repeating numbers, observing this phenomenon still has an effect. An invitation into to the higher angelic frequency, numbers expand consciousness from the soul level.

Angelic signs often bring us a sense peace, comfort, and love. They tend to come at times of loneliness, disappointment, or during, after, or before a challenging event or loss of some kind.

For instance, Ellen shared with me her miracle with the angels, as she liked to call it. It happened before her husband was about to go through a much-needed heart surgery. Although they knew the surgery was necessary, both Ellen and her husband were understandably nervous and anxious.

The night before her husband was to be admitted into the hospital, Ellen barely slept. Instead she silently lay in her bed, not wanting to wake her husband and for him to see her stress. Before dawn she slipped out of bed and went to sit on the back patio near the flower garden. As the sun slowly emerged, a small pink rose caught her eye. She watched in awe as it opened, petal by petal. As each petal unfurled and went from a closed bud to full bloom, her mind told her that this was not possible. Flowers do not, cannot open so quickly. Yet, as she allowed herself to accept the miracle that was happening in front of her eyes, she felt her heart open with calm assurance and peace. She knew that this was a sign. Her husband would come through the surgery just fine and he would soon be back on his feet. For a few more moments before waking him to go to the hospital, she sat with the miracle rose and thanked her angels for this gift and message.

The angelic realm works through the vibration and frequency of divine love, the energy of which bypasses human thinking and reasoning. If you encounter angelic signs, it is best to open your heart and become receptive. Resist the temptation to try to figure out why this is happening. You are simply ready to receive an angelic blessing. The timing of this may or may not make much sense to you. Your angels work through your heart and spirit. Listen within and trust your feelings and intuitive sense of knowing.

ARCHANGELS

Archangels are similar to angels in that they are pure emanations of divine presence. Archangels guide, protect, and influence events, and energetically promote and uphold principles such as justice, harmony, compassion, joy, and freedom. Change, activity, or circumstances that affect and influence collective consciousness or alter perceptions and beliefs are guided by archangels. However, archangels often send signs and messages to individuals. Normally this happens when someone has the opportunity to influence and guide others. People who work with the ill, the needy, and in environments where they can create change and impact others may be guided and supported by an arch-angel. In many spiritual traditions, revelations that have shifted mass consciousness and prevailing beliefs have been initiated by a message or sign from an archangel.

If you call on an archangel by name, or if you choose to live in ser-vice to the divine presence and be a blessing to others, archangels are with you and will send you messages, signs, and synchronicities.

For instance, Ted worked long hours for an investment firm. He attributed his success to a strong work ethic and his desire to help oth-ers. The financial rewards of his job allowed him the opportunity to travel and live in a beautiful home on a lake. Most weekends, pre-dawn, he and his wife would take the boat out and watch the sun come up. He looked forward to the day when he could retire and devote more time to fishing and relaxing in this way.

One afternoon after a quick trip out on the lake, he noticed a sud-den storm headed his way. He anchored the boat to the dock and while making his way to his backyard heard lightning strike. The loud boom rattled him and when he turned around to see what was hap-pening, lightning struck again. This time it seemed to lift him and then push him to the ground. Laying on the sand with rain pouring down on him, he wondered if he was hurt. Although he could move his limbs, he felt glued to the ground. A heavy force seemed to be weighing down on his chest. As he struggled to get up, he glanced at the lake and saw a rainbow of light in the distance that seemed out of place. Lightning and thunder still rained down on him and yet across the lake a sliver of sunlight on an arched rainbow glistened in the light. He felt his heart open and tears came to his eyes. Despite the fear and apprehension he felt, the beauty all around him was almost too much. His tears turned to sobs and he knew his purpose with clarity and certainty. He wouldn't wait for his retirement. For years he had helped people make money in ways that he knew was destroying the environment. He was harming what he most loved and he did not want to do it anymore. Ted knew that it was time to leave his job. If he was physically able to, he would give his notice on Monday. Now able to get up and make his way into his home, he made a vow that with the time he had have left on this earth he would do all that he could to heal the environment and protect the beauty of the land, sea, and skies.

SPIRIT GUIDES

Unlike angels and archangels, spirit guides have lived many lifetimes on earth. They are one of us. They have gone through similar kinds of challenges and lessons and have felt the same emotions we do. However, they no longer need to come back to the planet to continue their evolution. They have completed their earth life lessons and now they continue to grow and evolve in the spirit realm by helping and supporting those of us still on earth.

Some spirit guides tend to be interested in and focus on a specific area of your life. In one of their earth lives they may have had similar interests, expertise, gifts, and talents as you. Quite often we have shared a past life with a spirit guide and although on the human level we are not aware of it, we have a special bond of love with them.

For instance, Kurt knew that he needed to stop drinking. Once he started, he seemed to have no control, one drink led to another and another. As he looked back at his life, his drinking had destroyed so much of the good and left him with little. In the last few years, his girlfriend walked out on him, he was fired from two jobs, and he lost his driver's license.

After his last arrest for drunk driving, he was ordered to a treatment center. It was there that he started to attend daily AA meetings and his life began to turn around. Kurt felt that he was finally on track to becoming sober. A few of the people he met in AA introduced him to the idea of spirit guides, intuition, and the concept that he had a soul purpose. He liked these ideas and felt in his heart and gut that there was truth to them. Kurt was especially curious about spirit guides and wondered if he had one. With the encouragement of his friends, he sent a thought message to his spirit guide asking for help in discovering his purpose. He didn't know what to expect, but he felt that he had nothing to lose. If there was a purpose to his life, he wanted to know what it was.

A week or so later, while riding the subway on his way to an AA meeting, he overhead a conversation between two women talking about their children. One of the women was explaining how a new teacher was helping her son. From what Kurt caught in bits and pieces, the change in her son was almost miraculous. Hearing this story, Kurt remembered the positive difference a teacher made during a difficult period of his youth.

Later that day while running a few errands, he passed a school just as it was letting out for the day. As the students came streaming out, a woman came up to him and introduced herself. She told him that she was the mother of one of his students and she wanted to thank him for helping her son with a recent project. Kurt quickly told her that she was mistaken; he was just passing by the school and was not a teacher. She laughed and apologized and told him that he looked a lot like a teacher at the school.

These two coincidences or synchronicties on the same day got Kurt to thinking. When he shared these encounters with his friends, they thought this might be a sign from his spirit guide. They explained to him that sometimes the answers to our questions come in the form of synchronicities and other signs. With a warm feeling in his heart, Kurt recalled how he had wanted to be a teacher when he was younger. Kurt knew that he would need to go back to school and finish his degree and remain sober. He felt ready for this commitment and was excited by the prospect of improving himself and then being able to help others.

ASCENDED MASTERS

An ascended master is a spiritually enlightened being who has served humanity and now resides in the divine vibrations of love and wisdom where they continue to serve, help, heal, and enlighten souls in the physical and spiritual worlds. Some ascended masters, like Jesus, the Buddha, and Quan Yin are globally known and recognized. However, there are many ascended masters less known in the human world but no less devoted and powerful. They continue to actively transmit blessings and healing wherever it is needed.

When an ascended master sends you a sign, you know it. It can rattle you to the core and change your life forever. They don't play small. There signs are almost decrees. They come to inform us that it is time to change our lives, be of service, or wake up. Near death experiences, financial loss or gain, a profound dream, a heart opening, or illness are common signs from an ascended master. One of the ways that you know an ascended master has sent you a sign or message is by the indescribable feeling of love and holiness that accompanies them.

Although ascended masters work from the higher vibrations to affect and transform mass consciousness, they can be surprisingly intimate with helping us on an individual level. Many people have had encounters with ascended masters and received signs and messages from them.

When I was working on my book about Mother Mary, *The Miracle Workers Handbook*, I received many signs from her, some of which I wrote about in the book. In the years since its publication many people have contacted me to tell that they, too, have received signs and messages from Mary.

For instance, Sasha wrote to me that while reading the book she began to find white feathers. At first she did not think much of it, but when got in her car one morning and found a white feather on the console, she knew that Mother Mary had sent it to her. With her car parked in her garage and the doors locked, it would have been impossible, she told me, for anyone to have put the feather there. At the time this happened Sasha was working as a social worker case manager for mothers and families at risk. Her clients suffered abuse, poverty, and illness. Making little money and working long hours, her family and friends encouraged her to find other employment. She was considering taking their advice. Yet, in her heart she knew that she was where she wanted to be. When Sasha found the feather in her car, she knew that this was a sign from Mother Mary that she was fulfilling her divine purpose. She felt renewed and inspired to continue in her job.

LOVED ONES IN SPIRIT

Your loved ones on the other side are with you. They are still very much interested in your life and try to do all that they can to guide and comfort you. They love to send you signs to let you know that they are close. A loved one on the other side who shared a common interest, challenge, or personality trait with you may be surprisingly involved in your day-to-day affairs. During difficult times or when you are in need of comfort or guidance, your loved ones are especially present.

Common signs from loved ones include finding feathers or coins, hearing music that may have a special meaning or memory attached to it, encountering blooming flowers out of season, butterflies, or birds. You may smell the scent of their perfume or feel their warm touch on your hand or shoulder. A feeling of comfort and the sensation of heartfelt warmth may alert you to their presence. Because loved ones on the other side can influence energy flow, especially electricity, they often cause lights to flash, phones to ring, or buzzers to go off. They can knock things off of shelves, move small objects, and start and stop clocks. Your loved ones on the other side can have a lot of fun with these and other kinds of antics. It may take some practice for them to be able to effectively influence objects and materialize signs, but they love doing it.

It is not only the relatives and friends that you knew and were close to in the physical world that love and care for you. During medium readings, my clients are often surprised at who comes forward to communicate with them. It may be a grandfather that passed over before they were born, or an estranged aunt or uncle who is doing all that they can from the other side to be of help and assistance. I have worked with many adults who were adopted as babies and did not know their biological parents or their parents' families. Yet, almost always one of their biological parents, grandparents, or other family members comes through in a session to let my client know that they love and support them.

Quite often a family member who did not fulfill their responsibilities or acted in unloving and harmful ways will do all they can from the other side to support and help those who were hurt or negatively impacted by their actions. At times a parent, grandparent, or sibling with whom my client does not necessarily want to communicate may come into the session. When this happens I remind my clients that the intentions of the spirit realm are always pure and positive. Some of the greatest blessings that come into our life unknowingly come from those on the other side who are working hard to make up for their actions. Many hope that their loving grandmother or father will help them win the lottery or sell their house. Yet, it is more likely to be an alcoholic grandfather or ruthless ex-partner on the other side who is now influencing good fortune to come your way. Many signs, messages, and synchronicities that lead to abundance and positive outcomes may very well be coming from someone you least suspect.

Wanting to know that their loved ones are at peace and close by, many people ask for signs from their loved ones on the other side. Yet, as much as they hope to encounter one, nothing seems to come their way. This is what happened to Stella.

Her father died less than a year prior to our session. A spiritually attuned woman, she was distraught that she had not felt the presence of her father or received a sign from him since his passing. She came to see me to communicate with him and ask him why he had not paid her a visit.

Her father came forward as soon as I began the reading. Although she had not felt his presence, he shared a few observations about things currently going on in her life that reassured her that he was close. Toward the end of the session he told her to be careful for what she asked for. He would do his best to send her a sign that she would not miss. Stella laughed and told him that she would be waiting for an obvious sign from him.

"But please," she said, "no lizards."

From a young age, Stella had a fear of the small lizards that were common in the area where she grew up. Her father tried his best to help her to overcome her trepidation of them, but he was no help. Stella, now an adult, was still apprehensive around lizards.

When we finished the session, I walked into the waiting room with her. We were met by my next client coming up the stairs.

"A funny thing happened when I went to open your door," he said. "As I walked up the steps a large lizard climbed up on the door handle. I went back to my car and decided to wait there. Eventually I saw the lizard make its way up to the roof and took this opportunity to come in."

Stella and I looked at each other in awe and went to the front door. There was no lizard on it, but as we cautiously ventured out I noticed a large lizard staring down on us from the roof.

Your loved ones send signs your way for a variety of reasons. Sometimes they send signs just for fun and to let you know that they are close and they love you. At other times they may be trying to get you a message, comfort you, or help you to make a difficult decision or choice.

Nature Spirits and Spirit Power Animals

Within the natural world there are wise and highly evolved spirits that are guardians of the earth and all living creatures. Although spirit guides, angels, loved ones on the other side, and other spirit beings often send messages and signs through the natural world, nature spirits also offer their own guidance. A few of the most prominent types of nature spirits are fairies, devas, and spirit power animals.

Included within the fairy realm are sprites and pixies. They are legendary nature spirits who assist the earth in the changing seasons and watch over the animal and elemental kingdoms. Fairies assist the divine in bringing us signs, synchronicities, and messages. They are inhabitants of the divine realm most connected and intertwined within the physical and material vibration. This is also known as the fairy kingdom.

There are leagues of fairies who communicate with the upper levels of the divine, angels, spirit guides, and ascended masters, and carry out their wishes here on earth. Hardworking and always busy, they are powerful beings who are responsible for the surreal and hard-to-believe signs that you encounter. It is through their efforts that feathers fall on your path, the same bird continually sits on your windowsill, and flowers bloom out of season. They are also highly effective in working within urban environments to produce more contemporary signs. Fairies will at times initiate their own signs and messages, but they tell me that they are selective and like to mostly work with those who are committed to helping the natural world and the planet. However, they have a devotion to the spirit realm and work in unison with their wishes without reservation.

Devas

Devas are present within all aspects of nature. They are connected to the angelic realm and divine in nature. Without devas, the planet would be overwhelmed by the toxicity and pollution of human materialistic consumption and disregard. Balancing and harmonizing natural systems and processes, they keep the planet functioning and alive. Devas are present in the oceans, the forests, lakes, mountains, and clouds, and in the tiny bud of a flower. They align and support the elemental energies—fire, water, air, wood, and earth. The healing energy inherent within medicinal plants, vegetables, and fruit, and the nurturing energy of the animal kingdom, comes from devas.

You can feel the power of devas in the energy of a strong wind, a flowing river, or the pull of the ocean's tides. Grace and joy flow in grassy fields and emanates from a single rose or lily. They are hidden within the deep mystery of a full moon and the silent beauty of a sunrise or sunset. Devas can be benevolent and grace us with unspeakable natural beauty and healing or create havoc and chaos through destructive floods and earthquakes. When you experience the sun's warmth embracing you, the salty ocean spray tingling on your skin, or the changing color of leaves in the fall filling you with joy, you are being blessed by the divine healing energy of nature.

Power Animals

Another type of nature spirit is a spirit power animal. Just as we all have a spirit guide who watches over, guides, and protects us, so too do we have spirit power animals who are devoted guardians. Unlike the human realm, spirit power animals can inhabit the body of an animal in the physical world, then quickly shift back into nonphysical essence and spirit. Spirit power animals are not so much concerned with our ego wishes and goals, instead they inspire us to become aware of and integrate into our day-to-day lives our soul's timeless gifts and qualities. These may be attributes such as playfulness, healing abilities, strength, intuitive awareness, confidence, and compassion.

Spirit power animals often make contact with us through our dreams, sightings, finding feathers or paw prints, or through synchronicities. Dave, a college professor, told me that on his way to see me for a session a fox ran in front of his car. Surprised to see a fox in the middle of the day in a populated residential area, he realized that this was not the first fox he had seen in the past couple of weeks. While waiting for his wife in the car when she ran into a store, he spotted a fox in the woods near the parking lot. It silently stood still and seemed to be watching him.

"Does this mean something?" Dave asked me. "It seems more than a coincidence. I have never encountered a fox before. Now in less than two weeks, I have seen two of them. It doesn't seem possible. It feels like a message of some kind, but I'm not sure what it means. Can you help me to figure this out?"

As I intuitively tuned in to Dave's energy, I felt the presence of the fox. As a spirit power animal it had a lot to say.

"It seems that you have some pressure at work. The fox is here to help you move through the difficulties. The fox tells me that you would like to speak your truth but are hesitant to do this," I said.

Dave look startled and told me. "The department head doesn't share my philosophy. He would like me to adhere to his perspective when I teach, but I don't feel I can do that. It is a stressful situation. I don't want to lose my job. But I need to have integrity with my students."

"The fox is your ally. He is helping you to be adaptable, alert, and maneuver through this situation," I explained to Dave. "Even though he is not visible, he is with you at work, guiding and influencing you to be true to yourself."

YOUR HIGHER SELF

Our higher self is the most eternal and true aspect of who we are. It is aware of both our higher potential and purpose and our ego and personality self. The higher self can help guide us to positive opportunities and remind us of what is right and good for us. When we act from fear, self-centeredness, or in ways that go against our soul purpose and higher aims, the higher self sends us a message to get our attention. Common signs that come to us by way from our higher self to let us know that we are off track include such things as losing our keys, or jewelry such as a ring, getting lost when driving, or plans that suddenly fall apart.

When we notice and listen to the subtle signs that the higher self sends our way, we can avoid the change and upheaval that comes when we ignore messages from our spirit's command center. Although we tend to make decisions and choices based on our personality likes and dislikes and our wants and our needs, the higher self does not necessarily go along with this program.

Your higher self is your most authentic self. When you receive a sign or message from this part of you, it can feel familiar and obvious. So much so that we can ignore it. For instance, Keli had a decision to make. After working in the technology field for several years, she was contemplating taking the leap and starting a food business. Preparing food and cooking was where she felt most creative and alive. As far back as she could remember, she loved to mix ingredients and come up with new recipes. Family and friends raved about her abilities and often tried to hire her for small dinners and special occasions. Although she was doing well in her technology career, she often found herself daydreaming of running her own catering service, owning a food truck, or creating baked goods. Yet, leaving her secure job and steady income was not easy.

Although she tried to convince herself that she could continue to cook during her spare time, she started to become increasingly tired and depressed with the demands of her work. Like many people, she disregarded the initial signs of exhaustion and stress and continued to push through and keep working.

One evening after a ten-hour work day, while making her way through heavy and slow traffic, she found herself behind a bus. On the back of the bus was a large sign that read, *Create Your Dream*. Keli stayed behind this bus for the next couple of miles before turning off to her street. At every stop and start the sign seemed to speak to her. Although it was an ad for a local college, she knew the message was meant for her. As she pulled into her driveway, Keli realized that it was time to create her dream. She could make a food business work. She felt it in her heart and soul. That evening she stayed up late into the night writing down a business plan and putting together all the information she felt she would need to begin to create her dream.

Your higher self will send you guiding signs that point you in the right direction. Often these signs are experienced in the outer world as opportunities, unexpected financial gain, or unexpected positive change in our circumstances. These events come with feelings of positivity and joy and the inner knowing that we need to take a leap and act on what has come into our lives. The higher self often uses signs that have meaningful significance. Hearing a song that may have been popular and important during a pivotal time in your life, or spontaneously recalling a memory that triggers forgotten aspects of your true self and reminds you of what is truly important, are signs from your higher self.

Although it is not aways important or necessary to know who is sending you a sign or message, it can be helpful in interpreting its meaning. It is not likely that you will have verifiable proof of who or what has sent you a sign. Trust your intuition, inner feelings, and sense of knowing without overfocusing. Sometimes when we least expect it, the awareness of who is close and communicating with us suddenly becomes clear.

CHAPTER 4

TYPES OF SIGNS

Sacred signs and messages often come to us without any effort on our part. They appear during times of calm and peace, when we feel lonely and lost, during difficulties, when we have a choice or decision to make, and often when we least expect them. Although you may not initially understand a sign and even wonder if you are imagining things, there is always purpose and meaning within signs and messages.

Here are some of the most common types of signs.

I AM HERE SIGNS

The divine spirit realm often sends us signs and messages just to let us know that they are with us. Angels, loved ones on the other side, nature spirits, and spirit guides can be quite sociable and have many ways of letting us know that they are close. Some signs may be easily recognizable, like finding feathers or coins, or seeing rainbows, butterflies, birds, heart-shaped clouds, or flowers. Some signs are more personal, such as spotting a frog-shaped pendant like the one your mother used to wear in a store window on the anniversary of her passing.

Loved ones on the other side are especially determined to let us know that they are close. They may blink the lights in your house or even the streetlights as you walk down the street. They can start and stop clocks or timers, interrupt service on your cellphone or computer WiFi, and generally wreak havoc through influencing electrical currents. They also send many personal messages that only we may understand.

For instance, before I shut the door behind her, my client Sarah sat down and began talking. "I was walking through the botanical gardens a few weeks ago," she said. "There were just a few other people there. It was early morning and I was watching the ducks. I started to hear music. It sounded familiar. Then I realized it was coming from my phone in my pocket. I thought that I must have somehow accidentally turned it on as I was walking. I didn't think too much of it."

Sarah inched her way forward on the couch, closer to me, as she continued. "Well, a week or so later I went for another walk in the gardens and almost in the same spot that my phone began to play music a week or so earlier, I heard music again. This seemed a little too odd. I could see if my phone did this all the time, but it doesn't. I can't recall it ever doing it before," she said.

"I thought it was probably just one of those strange synchronicties. Then I started thinking about my mother's upcoming birthday. She would have been eighty this year. She passed over ten years ago. It feels like it was just yesterday. Then I remembered how much she loved walking in the botanical gardens. As I thought of her, a soothing wave of warmth and love moved through me. I could almost feel her next to me."

SIGNS OF CHANGE

Signs and messages often come to us to announce change or to motivate us to create change. Being patient and knowing when to take action and when to wait is one of the more subtle but difficult lessons that we are learning here in the physical realm. In the spirit world time does not exist in the same way that it does here. In spirit there is only now, the eternal moment. Although it may not seem like one of the bigger challenges we may encounter, most people I work with struggle with timing in some way. When something that we have worked hard to accomplish or manifest does not happen in the way and time that we expect it to, we can become anxious and confused. We may question our effort, our worthiness, others' actions and input, and, even at times, the existence of God. Alternatively, sometimes we wait and do nothing. We expect that what we desire will show up when we want it to, but it never seems to happen. We become lazy and complacent with inertia.

Change signs can be helpful and inspiring. They can encourage us to become aware of when we need to take action and assure us when something is coming our way.

This is what happened to Brittany. Living alone after a difficult divorce, she was rebuilding her life as best she could. The part-time job she had while married was not enough to financially support her. With no full-time positions available at her current job, she began searching for work. After months of going on interviews and sending out her résumé, she was becoming discouraged. The initial feeling of elation when her divorce was finalized was also fading. She was lonely, anxious, and not sleeping well. To soothe her nerves she started praying before going to sleep at night. Not religious or especially spiritual, she told me that she didn't direct her prayers to anyone in particular.

"I want to cover all my bases," she said. "I just ask for whatever and whoever to help me. But I do it with a lot of gusto. I really need divine intervention."

One morning as she got in her car to go to work, Brittany noticed a ballon on a string wrapped around one of her bushes. Sprawled across the balloon were the words, *Congratulations! It's a Girl!* She smiled and laughed when she saw it and felt that perhaps this was a positive omen.

When she arrived at work she was met by her supervisor. He asked her into his office and explained that he had been meaning to speak to her for a few days. A full-time position had opened up in her department and he wanted to give her the first option in accepting it.

Change signs often come as opportunities and invitations to try something we have always wanted to do or planned to do but never got around to it. They can also signal us when it is time to take action.

For example, for over two years, Ted had been working part-time as a holistic healer, a far departure from his full-time job as a software engineer. His plan was to transition out of the software job and into his healing work full time. After setting a date and doing the preliminary work of getting everything in order, he found himself unsure if it was the right time. Even though he had plenty of clients and a waiting list for his services, the date that he had originally planned on came and went. Months later and exhausted from working days as an engineer and nights as a healer, he still had not taken the leap to work full-time in his healing practice.

One morning while walking his dog, a large owl swooped close over him. For a moment the owl's wide wingspan spread hovered over him and his heart leapt. Symbolic of intuition, he realized that the owl was a sign that he needed to better listen to and pay attention to his inner voice. He wanted logical and verifiable proof that he could work fulltime in his healing practice. It was time; he knew to trust his heart and gut and take the step.

GUIDANCE SIGNS

When we are confronted with a decision or choice, or when we would like the advice of a higher love and wisdom, we often look to signs for guidance and direction. All oracles were developed for this purpose. We have a barometer-like inner knowing that motivates and assures us that there is a universal benevolent and guiding force that responds to our needs.

In ancient times when someone noticed a spontaneous sign, they paid attention to current and future conditions, events, and changes. It was through this kind of close observation that meaning was attributed to specific signs and natural occurrences, and oracles were developed. We still notice these kinds of connections. For instance, a friend of mine knows that her grandfather is sending her a message when she finds dimes. A single mother raising two children, she feels the dimes are a signal to pay attention to her finances and how she is spending money. If she is contemplating a big purchase she feels the dimes are telling her to slow down and rethink before buying. She has successfully used this strategy for years in purchases, and investments.

Guidance signs often spontaneously surface when we are in need of direction. Quite often these messages come in a form that we already associate with meaning. For instance, we may have a positive association with specific numbers. The numbers 1, 2, 7, or repetitions and combinations of these numbers are for many positive signs. The numbers 13, 666, or 5 may have more cautious or negative associations. Different cultures attribute different meaning and significance to certain numbers. For instance, in China the numbers 2, 8, and 9 are considered positive omens, while the number 4 is thought to be unlucky. In India a number ending with the numeral 1 is considered lucky.

Noticing repeating numbers or specific patterns of numbers often occurs when we are undergoing or about to undergo transformation and change of some kind. This is what happened to Lily. Although she was looking forward to her youngest child leaving home to go to college, she didn't know what it would be like to not have a child in the house. The first few weeks went by quickly. She rearranged some furniture, did some painting, and went out to dinner with friends. A single parent for many years, she had built her life around her children, and now that they were off living their lives, she wondered who she was and where she was going.

"This is when I started to see the number 1:11 or 11:11," Lily told me. "I woke up one night at 1:11 and didn't think too much of it. Then the next day, when I glanced at the clock at 1:11, I thought it was just a quirky coincidence. Now, a day doesn't go by without the numbers 1 or 11 showing up in some way. What is going on?" She asked.

I explained to Lily that seeing the repeating number 1 is a sign from the angelic realm. Her angels were letting her know that they were guiding her. These numbers were her assurance that even though she did not have a clear sense of the future, she was on the right track.

In addition to numbers, many have a positive connection to specific birds or other natural elements. Seeing butterflies, hawks, robins, or hummingbirds may help you to make a decision or guide you in a certain direction.

Guidance signs often come through synchronicities. If you are confused or confronting a choice, pay attention to unexpected encounters, chance meetings, and coincidences. Guidance messages include such things as being given or coming across a book or article or overhearing a conversation or discussion that seems to speak to or provide insight into a current question or concern.

For instance, while waiting to be seated in a restaurant, Carol, a client of mine, overheard two women in the line behind her discussing a cruise that one of them had been on a few weeks prior. Contemplating taking her family on a cruise to the same destination that the two women talked about, she intently listened. As she did she heard glowing reports about the great food, accommodations, and the spectacular beauty that they encountered on the cruise. Carol felt that this was no accident; she felt that this was a sign and later that day booked the cruise.

Like comfort signs, guidance signs may appear before we recognize a need for them. Your higher self, spirit guides, and ascended masters are particularly skilled at sending messages to you through your day-to-day routines, experiences, and encounters. Plans that suddenly fall through, opportunities that either fail to deliver or provide unexpected gain, and being laid off or being surprised with an unanticipated job offer are often guidance messages pointing us in the right direction for our highest good.

WARNING SIGNS

Warning signs emerge when we are not listening and paying attention to our inner self or more subtle messages. When we want to push through something, become inflamed with desire, or when we are heading into a situation that can cause us harm, warning messages often come our way. Many of my clients have shared stories of warning signs. The most dramatic of which involve warnings that have saved them from tragedy and loss.

For instance, I have a client who was scheduled to be on one of the flights involved in the September 11 attacks. The night before her flight she had a dream that her grandfather was shaking her out of a sound sleep. She woke up and for the rest of the night could not fall back to sleep. Finally, close to dawn she closed her eyes and started to drift off. Again, she felt herself being shaken out of a deep sleep. Exhausted and rattled by the dreams, she called her office and postponed her trip. A few hours later, the plane that she was meant to be on crashed into one of the towers.

Warning signs can be confusing. Everything in your life may seem normal and uneventful, then out of nowhere a sign appears that makes no sense. Common warning signs include such subtle occurrences as repeatedly having to stop at red lights while driving, getting lost, taking a wrong turn that ends up being a dead end, losing your keys, being locked out of your house, getting flat tires, having phones that break, have delayed planes, or missing appointments. Anything that forces you to pause or slow down and ask, *what is going on,* can be a warning sign. If you encounter these and other similar kinds of situations and conditions that hamper your progress and cause inconvenience, they are no accident. It is important to recognize and acknowledge them. Stop and contemplate your current plans and direction.

There are, however, other less obvious warning signs that may only make sense to you. Whenever I find a bluejay feather, I know that something is not right. This is my warning sign. When I encounter a bluejay feather, I am especially alert and aware. However, it took a few years of observation to fully recognize their meaning. The pivotal experience that revealed their meaning occurred one summer morning when I found a dead bluejay near my front door. When I saw the beautiful and elegant bird I immediately felt a wave of sadness and loss and an impending sense of doom. Not long after this, my mother was diagnosed with terminal cancer.

Later that year, I found a bluejay feather and then another one. For a few weeks I seemed to find bluejay feathers almost every day. Not long after this, I found out that the man that I was dating was also seeing someone else. Ever since these incidents, I pay special attention when I come across bluejay feathers. They have not failed to warn and motivate me to pay attention, and to let me know when something is not what it appears to be.

ReDirection Signs

Have you ever made plans, been meticulous with detail, did all that you could do to assure a successful trip, project, or venture and something comes out of nowhere to change everything? For instance, maybe you have an interview for a new job that looks perfect. On your way there you get a flat tire, end up arriving late and disheveled, and the job goes to someone else. When things like this happen, we are usually disappointed and confused at our bad luck. Usually it is only in retrospect that we appreciate and can make sense of the hidden blessings within an unfortunate or confusing event.

There are unseen, wise, and powerful forces at work in the universe that set up experiences and situations to help us discover our true self, evolve, and ultimately experience more joy. When we are off track or going counter to what is essential for our soul purpose and plan, signs may come our way to reroute us. We are seldom fully aware of the extent that we are being guided and influenced.

For instance, from a young age Jerry wanted to be a farmer. Growing up in an urban area and the son of a schoolteacher and an engineer, no one took this dream seriously. Even so, when he was young he made the best use of the small plot of sunny land in his backyard to grow a few vegetables. When he asked for a goat for his tenth birthday, his father rolled his eyes and instead gave him a new video game.

Over time, Jerry's dream of becoming a farmer was sidelined by school, sports, and eventually college. After graduating with a degree in business, he got a job in the human resources department of a local company. After working there for a few years, he saved enough money for a down payment on a home. Everyone, himself included, assumed that he would then marry his girlfriend and start a family. Everything seemed to be on track.

But as is often the case, there was another plan for his life. Driving home from work one day in heavy traffic he was detoured through a part of town that he seldom frequented. Moving slowly, he came to a stop in front of a grocery store that was advertising locally grown organic vegetables. Remembering his dream to be a farmer, he recalled the passion and enthusiasm he had for growing carrots and radishes in the backyard. For the rest of the drive home he reminisced about his long-term interest in farming. To his surprise the passion and desire for farming was still very much alive within him. As he pulled into his driveway, he noticed a flyer stuck in his front door. When he opened it, the words *Live Your Passion!* leapt out at him. The flyer was advertising the opening of a new arts school in the area, but in his heart he knew that this was a sign.

"I want to be a farmer," he said out loud to himself, surprised by the conviction he felt. "I really want to be a farmer. That is what I am here to do."

When his girlfriend came home from work he shared with her his desire to farm. She was enthusiastic and shared that she, too, wanted to live closer to the earth and was on board in working toward this goal.

However, not all rerouting signs are met with this much enthusiasm. They might also invoke frustration and disappointment. When you feel that you are encountering one obstacle after another, or that plans are continually met with opposition, it may be time to take a step back and be patient. Give yourself some time and space and listen to your intuition. When something is meant to be, there is a sense of support and ease through which it unfolds. You may still need to work hard and focus, but you make progress and receive positive results.

Other common rerouting signs are encountering road detours or road blocks, documents or information being lost in the mail or cyberspace, computer malfunctions, and being offered unexpected opportunities.

COMFORT SIGNS

Some signs help us to feel a sense of comfort and connection with a loved one on the other side, an angel, or a spiritual presence. They provide us with the assurance that we are being watched over and are not alone. These signs often have personal significance and often induce feelings of heart-opening warmth and may even bring us to tears. Common examples of comfort signs include hearing music that has special meaning or memories attached to it, smelling the perfume, aftershave, or a tobacco scent reminiscent of a loved one on the other side, or spontaneously receiving a much-wanted desire or wish.

Comfort signs usually occur during times of stress, loss, difficulties, or emotional or physical illness. Speaking directly to the heart, we may quickly notice, trust, and feel solace and peace. Although we often receive comfort signs after the passing of a loved one or during or after an unexpected change in life circumstances, like the end of a marriage or the loss of a job, it is possible to receive them during periods of calm tranquility. Some comfort signs occur before a coming event or situation and it may be only after a loss or stressful event that we recognize the significance of what we previously experienced. The spirit realm knows what is coming our way and is with us, offering support and strength even before an event occurs.

For instance, one evening while reading before heading to bed, Char smelled the familiar flowery scent of her grandmother. A bit surprised, she sat back and felt her heart fill with warmth and love. A minute or so later, she went back to reading her book. The words that jumped off the page startled her. In her novel, the young heroine discovered her lover has taken his life in a tragic suicide. A chill ran up her spine. Char tried to brush away the thought that feeling the presence of her grandmother and reading this passage were somehow connected.

However, a few days later, Char's son called and in tears told her that he had just found out that an ex-girlfriend had taken her life. Later that evening after making plane reservations to visit her son, she thought of her encounter with her grandmother a few nights earlier. It now made more sense. Her grandmother had come to let her know that she was watching over her son. Not only did this bring her a sense of comfort, she knew that Katy, his ex-girlfriend, was being watched over and helped as well. Closing her eyes, she prayed for her son and Katy, and sent gratitude to her grandmother for her love and comfort.

Some comfort signs are not in response to an actual event or condition but speak to our worries and stress. For instance, Pat's son Kal was diagnosed with autism when he was in elementary school. With support from his family, counselors, therapists, and schools, he graduated from high school and was accepted into college. The college he attended was several hours from home and Pat was nervous and anxious about her son living on his own.

Soon after Pat's second trip to visit Kal, she sent me an e-mail with a photo attached to it. In the photo was a truck with the word KAL, emblazoned in bold letters on the back of it. Pat explained that on her first trip to see her son, she noticed that she was driving behind a car with the letters KAL on it license plate. Now, after spotting her son's name on the back of this vehicle, he knew that it was more than a co-incidence. When I asked her what she thought it meant she told me that she believed that it was a message from her angels, assuring her that they were watching over her son. She told me that this has brought her unimaginable comfort and peace.

HEALING SIGNS

Healing signs come to us in times of need, illness, grief, or as an an-swer to prayer. Although they may not be as obvious as some of the other types of signs, it is not so much the outer form of the sign that is significant but the effect and influence that it provides. All signs are inherently capable of providing healing as they are created from di-vine source energy. What differentiates a healing sign from others is that they appear when physical, mental, emotional, or spiritual heal-ing and renewal is needed.

For instance: Ellen, a single woman in her late fifties, struggled with long-term Lyme disease. Although she had experienced almost constant joint pain and exhaustion, she had no choice but to work every day. One morning it all felt like too much. She took to her bed and had no energy to get up. A couple of days later, still lying in bed, she woke to the sound of a bird singing. She went to her window and noticed a cardinal sitting on a nest in a small tree branch against her window. As she watched the cardinal she noticed another one, singing from another branch close by. She lay back down, feeling soothed and comforted.

For the next few days Ellen heard the bird's gentle song and watched the devoted birds tending to their not-yet-born offspring. Lying in bed half asleep she felt and imagined herself being tended to with the same kind of love and devotion.

One early morning she woke to the sound of soft chirping. She went to the window and was greeted by three little beaks peeking out of the nest. As she sat watching the proud parents tend to their babies, she felt surprisingly stronger and happy. For the first time in over a week, Ellen felt like getting dressed and doing some errands.

"It's funny," she thought to herself, "I feel like I am ready to flee the nest too."

When she opened the front door on her way to work a few days later, she noticed a single bright red cardinal feather on her stoop. She picked it up and knew it was a sign that she was being watched over and healed.

Healing signs can also inspire and motivate us to seek out a particular doctor or healer, or provide us with information about a problem or condition that we are experiencing. Common signs include synchronicities that involve hearing the name of a healthcare practitioner or a specific treatment, or having a chance meeting with someone who has or is close to another who has successfully treated the same condition or issue that we are experiencing. Signs that you are healing and signs that bring the assurance that you are on the road to recovery include such things a seeing a rainbow, blooming flowers (especially off-season), or encountering fountains, waterfalls, or steams or rivers with pure, clear water.

When you allow yourself to fully embrace signs and messages, you may find that the conditions, stress, or worry that has been plaguing you transforms. Signs and synchronicities embody high-vibration life force energy. In the midst of a sign or synchronicity, many experience waves of love that seem to move through the body and soul, or feelings of warmth and compassion that open the heart. Not only do these feelings signal the presence of a higher love and wisdom, they can also create significant shifts in our perspective, provide new insights, and heal feelings of loneliness, grief, and loss. This happens quite often when a loved one from the other side sends us signs and messages.

For instance, after Jody's mother died she felt herself slip into the depths of despair and grief. As much as she tried to work through her feelings of loss and sadness, heavy emotions seemed to hang over her like a heavy shroud. Nothing seemed to be able to heal her depression. One morning while getting ready for work, she found a necklace of her mother's in her top drawer. Perplexed as to how it may have gotten there, she felt a shiver of warmth move through her heart as she held it in her hand. Suddenly it felt as if her mother was with her. She felt the sensation of a hand on her shoulder and remembered her mother's laugh. In this moment of connection with her mother's spirit, she felt the grief fall away.

DECISIONS, FINANCES, AND RELATIONSHIP SIGNS

When we are undergoing difficulties or facing challenges in the everyday areas of finances and relationships, or when we need to make a decision, helpful signs and messages often spontaneously emerge. When in need of specific guidance in one of these areas, be on the lookout for these symbols and signs.

Decision-Making Signs

If you are making a decision that requires a *yes* or *no* response, there are a few signs that may help to guide you. Common *yes* signs include such things as a series of green streetlights, an upright ladder, finding coins, flowing water, encountering a pregnant woman, the color green or gold, a windmill, a flock of birds flying overhead in the direction you are walking, or an "Open" sign on a business, store, or public place.

Common signs that may indicate *no* or *do not go forward* include signs such as a "No Exit," "Do Not Enter," or "Out of Business." Encountering a growling dog, hearing of a death, the wind blowing against you, a series of red lights, a dried stream or fountain with no water, a dead-end road, and a fallen bird's nest may also indicate not moving forward with a plan or idea.

Finances and Abundance Signs

Positive financial and abundance signs include such things as blooming flowers, light rain, sun showers, finding coins or money, birds singing, rainbows, fruit trees, or flowing water or fountains.

Signs that may signify financial loss or lack include such things as potholes in the street, holes of any kind, storms, withering trees or flowers, being asked for money, fruit trees or berry bushes with rotting or no fruit, or fountains or streams with little or no water.

Relationship Signs

Patterns of two, and the activity between two things, such as two birds, trees, dogs, children, or people, provide insight into relationship issues.

Positive signs include such interactions as two children playing or laughing, a couple holding hands or kissing, or two birds playing or singing. Other positive relationship signs may emerge through synchronicities that involve even numbers, complete circles, or red flowers in bloom.

Less positive signs may be two people arguing, children not getting along, or dogs growling at one another. If you encounter single items or people, such as one person walking alone, one dog or child, or one tree standing alone, or a single car in a parking lot, this may indicate being alone or on your own.

The weather often reveals relationship signs and messages. The sun peeking through dark clouds or a warm, gentle breeze on a cool day are messages of an improving relationship. A sudden storm, a strong wind, or freezing rain may be messages of relationship disharmony and difficulties.

For instance, Paula, a friend of mine, went through a difficult breakup with her longtime boyfriend. She was blindsided by his abrupt announcement one Sunday morning that he was no longer in love with her. Paula grieved the end of this relationship for many months and had little motivation to get out and meet new people. One afternoon about a year after her breakup, she bumped into an old high school boyfriend while she was getting her car washed. She had not seen Bradly in several years, and as they caught up with one another, she sensed that there was still a spark between them. Later that week, he called and asked if he could take her out to dinner. Having gone through a divorce about a year ago, he was ready to start dating again. Paula's initial reaction was to say no to his invitation. While she was admittedly attracted to him, she didn't know if she was ready to date.

As they continued to talk on the phone, a ray of sunlight hit her through the window. It had been cloudy, cold, and overcast for most of the week and the sunlight felt warm and relaxing. Something in her knew that this was a sign. The warmth of the sun seemed to reach down and open her heart. Later that week, she and Bradly had dinner and a few years later they married.

———

These are just a few of the varied ways that the divine spirit realm and your own soul reach out to you through signs, messages, and synchronicities. Keep in mind that you may experience a sign or message that is not necessarily one of these types of signs or one that seems to speak to more than one category.

CHAPTER 5

SIGN MAPPING

To use signs, messages, and synchronicities for guidance and direction it is important to develop a relationship and familiarity with them. There are a few common characteristics that signs share. As you become more aware of the events surrounding their appearance and how and when they surface, they will become more frequent.

It can be helpful to keep a journal and document your encounters and experiences with signs and messages to better notice patterns and commonalities. As you do this you will become more comfortable deciphering their symbolic meaning, and your ability to gain insight into their message will become more spontaneous and natural.

NOTICING SIGNS

When Sheila left her office to take a quick trip to the post office, she noticed two doves sitting on a branch near the entrance. If it hadn't been for the cooing that startled her, she would have never noticed them. On her way back to the office Sheila was waiting for a light to turn green when two small sparrows that were playfully chasing one another flew directly in front of her car windshield. When she noticed these two birds, a warm flow of energy filled her heart while a shiver of energy moved up her spine, and an image of the single and good-looking man that she had recently met at a friend's home came to mind. She smiled when she thought of him. However, by the time she pulled up into the parking lot at work, she had forgotten all about the birds and warm feelings she had recently experienced.

Divorced for several years, Sheila was beginning to doubt if she would ever meet her soulmate. If she had been more alert to and aware of signs, she might have recognized the birds as important messangers bringing the news that a positive relationship was on its way. The more we engage with signs, the easier it becomes to decipher them.

Here are some questions that will help you to be alert to signs and get the most from them:

- Do I notice signs and synchronicities, or do they seem to happen more to others and not me?
- Am I initially trusting and excited when I encounter a sign, but then become more skeptical and doubtful?
- When I receive a sign, am I grateful and open-hearted, or do I question and dismiss it?
- When I encounter a sign, can I pause and listen within to my intuition?
- Are there any bodily sensations, a sense of warmth, or emotions and feelings that accompany signs?
- Do I feel the presence of angels or loved ones on the other side when I encounter a sign?
- Do signs seem to trigger my intuitive awareness? Do I sometimes receive instantaneous insights and revelations?
- Do I feel loved, comforted, restored, or healed during or after receiving a sign, omen, or synchronicity?

Asking yourself these questions and journaling your responses will help you to notice signs, increase your intuitive receptivity, and gain insight into their meaning and deepen your overall experience.

WHAT'S HAPPENING

Working at technology firm for the past several years was no longer enjoyable for Laura. She thought long and hard about what she really wanted to do and accomplish. She kept imagining herself going back to school and getting a teaching degree in special education. Yet, she feared that she was being impractical and overly idealistic. She didn't know what to do.

One morning the train she was on that took her into the city for work unexpectedly stopped. She heard an announcement that a small mechanical issue was at fault but that they would soon be up and moving. She glanced out the window and noticed that the train had stopped in front of a schoolyard. Children were busy going into the school and she noticed a pretty little girl in a wheelchair smiling and laughing with some others girls while being escorted into the school. In her heart she knew that this was more than a coincidence. It was a sign that becoming a teacher was the right decision for her; she was sure of it.

It can be helpful to pay attention to the circumstances and conditions that you are experiencing when you encounter a sign. This will help you to better tune in to its message and what it is related to. Ask yourself these questions when you encounter a sign:

- Am I lonely and in need of comfort?
- Is there a choice or decision I am confronting?
- Have I been thinking of a loved one on the other side?
- Have I sent a message or prayer to my angels or the divine presence asking for guidance and direction?
- Am I experiencing a new beginning in my life, planning a trip, starting a new job, or beginning a new relationship?
- Does the presence of a sign coincide with an anniversary, birthday, or special past event?

Not only are present-time conditions important, but what unfolds after you receive a sign is equally significant. Here are some questions to ponder after you have received a sign

- Has something unexpected occurred after I received a sign or experienced a synchronicity?
- Has a new opportunity presented itself?

- Has a relationship ended or a new one begun? Has there been any change in my finances, either loss or gain, or surprising opportunity?
- Has there been a birth, illness, healing, or passing over soon after the emergence of a sign or synchroncity?

PATTERNS

Jessie was getting ready for a fun weekend with some old college friends when the lights in his apartment flickered. He didn't think too much of it. When he got back on Monday, he thought, he would make a report to the office and ask them to check it out. This was the third time it had happened in the last couple of days.

That evening he met up with his friends in the sports bar near their old college dorm. They were having a great time and in an unusual pause in the conversation the lights of the bar flickered. That's odd, he thought, and shared with his friends how the lights in his apartment had also begun to flicker. One by one his old college friends shared the same story. In the last few days they had all noticed the lights in their homes or offices quickly going off and on again.

Jessie didn't know if it was the alcohol talking, but he quickly thought of Jerry. He had attended college with this group and had died in a car accident on spring break during his senior year. Jokingly, Jessie mentioned to the group that maybe Jerry was letting them know that he was with them. Surprisingly, his friends shook their heads in agreement. It would be just like Jerry, they reasoned. He never wanted to miss out on a good time, they reminisced. They bought another round and made a toast to their good friend.

Signs can be repetitive. Notice signs that repeat themselves or patterns that continually surface. As you do this, their meaning and message will become more apparent and clear. Here are a few questions to help you develop a better understanding of the meaning of specific signs:

- Does unexpected financial gain or loss repeatedly occur after an encounter with a specific sign?

- Do the lights in my home flicker or my phone mysteriously ring when I am thinking or talking about a loved one who has passed over?
- Do I glance at a clock or watch at the same time, day and night?
- Do I continually find feathers from the same species of bird, for instance, bluejay, owl, or hawk?
- Do I often find the same denomination of coin, for instance pennies, nickels, dimes, or quarters?

SYMBOLIC SIGNIFICANCE

Jenni was twenty-four years old. The number on the house that she grew up in was twenty-four. She was also born in February, the second month of the year, on the fourth. Her license plate even had a twenty-four in it. There was no doubt in her mind—when the number 24 surfaced, she paid attention.

Since graduating from college, Jenni had not been able to find a job that she liked. She felt as if she was just floating along with no goals and no destination. Some days she felt invisible and did not know what to do with herself. On what seemed like an endless job search, she scanned her notes for the address of the next job interview.

The office was hard to find, but eventually she sat in the waiting area, not very hopeful that the job would work out. A friend of hers had gotten her the interview, and although she would love to work in television production, she was used to disappointments. After being called in for the interview, she nervously sat in front of the production manager and listened to what he was looking for. Jenni was startled when she heard that there was more than one job opening and that one of them was for a new division called 7/24. She had always had a thing for numbers and considered the number 7 her lucky number, and of course 24 was her number. She knew she would get the job, and she did.

Perceiving the world and what you experience in a symbolic way is an ability that may take practice, attentive observation, and the ability to employ creative, intuitive thinking. Here are some questions to ask yourself:

- Do certain songs, movies, or pieces of art invoke deep emotions or remind me of another time or certain people from the past?
- Can I make associations between what I am experiencing and the signs that I encounter?
- Are there certain things that I encounter that remind me of something from my past or invoke a memory?
- Do I pay attention to my dreams and seek to understand their meaning?
- Do I look beyond appearances and penetrate to the core of an issue or situation?
- Do certain numbers, colors, or objects have symbolic meaning to me?

When you experience a sign, take note of anything that you notice or feel, even if it does not seem particularly important. Your awareness of subtle clues and connections will become more obvious as you focus attention on them. In time, the meaning behind the message will likely become more clear. Keep in mind that some signs, synchronicities, and messages bypass human reasoning. Not every sign will be intellectually understood and make sense. This does not mean that it has no purpose or meaning. Instead, the divine energy inherent within the sign is working on an unconscious level. Healing, transformation, and consciousness growth cannot always be understood on a rational and human level.

PART 2
THE LIVING ORACLE

Sacred signs, messages, and synchronicities offer us helpful and enlightening guidance and insight. Given their benefit and their ability to help us to experience a closer connection to a greater power and presence, there likely will be times when you may want to invoke them.

In this section you will learn how to invoke and interpret signs and messages as an oracle. Depending on your concerns, questions, and the kind of guidance that you would like to receive, there are several different oracles and divination methods to choose from.

CHAPTER 6
WORKING WITH THE LIVING ORACLE

When it comes to looking to sacred signs and messages for guidance and direction, we are not too different from our ancestors. In the pattern of moss on rocks, a tree branch swaying in a certain direction, or the sudden appearance of an animal, past cultures were guided to do such things as choose a leader, plant crops, or go to war. Spontaneously occurring signs and messages became so vital to ancient civilizations, systems to invoke them were created. With the ability to observe signs and connect them to present conditions and upcoming changes, accurate oracles were devised, several of which are still in use thousands of years later.

Oracle systems provide beneficial guidance and wisdom. They help us to understand the unknown influences as work in our lives, offer insights into ourselves and others, and empower us to become aware of upcoming changes. The Living Oracle is a system through which you can invoke signs and messages for general guidance, for a concern or question, or for insight into a particular area of your life.

CASTING THE LIVING ORACLE

Invoking signs and messages through a Living Oracle exercise is referred to as casting the oracle. There are six Living Oracle options to choose from: Sign Signature, Temple of Spirit, Sign Medicine Wheel,

Sign Walkabout, Sign Sanctuary, and Sign Vision Quest oracles. Each of these oracles is cast in a slightly different way.

Casting a Living Oracle is a communication and dialogue with invisible forces and with the world around you. Igniting your personal power and awakening you to the magic hidden within the mundane and everyday, casting the oracle places you in the center of its activity.

The process begins by asking for the presence of a higher power of love and wisdom to guide and direct the oracle. This higher power may be your own soul and higher self. The heavens and divine forces open wide when we make a sincere request.

In most of the Living Oracle exercises, you do not need to ask for a specific spiritual presence or know the name of a spirit guide or angel. However, if you have a loved one on the other side you would like to hear from, or would like guidance from an angel or spirit guide, you can ask for their presence to guide the oracle. This is a personal process through which you can invoke and ask for guidance from whatever or whoever you are most comfortable with and believe in. Simply sending a sincere message from the heart will be felt and heard. Before you cast the oracle, it is helpful to take a few moments to focus on your concern or the area of your life where you would like guidance and direction. However, you can also cast the oracle for general guidance or for comfort and connection with the spirit realm. It is important to note that the oracle you cast may not address your question or concern, but instead speak to another aspect of your life. Whatever you are feeling strongly about or undergoing creates a strong energy attraction and will draw signs and messages to you. If the signs that you receive seem to be addressing another issue in your life or bringing up a topic that you did not seek guidance on, go with it. There may be important guidance presented that will be helpful in some way.

Your attitude in casting the oracle will affect its outcome. It is important to trust that there is a presence and power that exists outside of the boundaries of material laws, and this presence can and will direct and influence what you encounter. It is normal and natural to have doubts. You are stepping outside of the three-dimensional paradigm of logic and reason. Cultivate an open heart and mind and a sense of wonder that allows for possibilities and the element of surprise.

LIVING ORACLE SIGNS

Unlike other types of divination systems that may use cards, coins, or runes, in the Living Oracle you cast yourself into the environment to observe and detect signs and messages.The Living Oracle was created to be practiced primarily in urban areas, towns, cities, suburbs, and residential areas. Within the everyday activity of urban settings, a higher presence can influence the environment and speak to you.

Because many early oracle systems that involve signs were created at a time when we lived closer to nature, they predominantly focus on signs within the natural world. While such living things as birds, trees, and animals are included within the Living Oracle, there are also many other common objects and things that you may encounter that are potential signs and messages.

This includes such things as:

- Activities involving others
- Buildings
- Places of business
- Roads and road conditions
- Street signs
- The weather
- Vehicles

The oracle's basic parameters are defined by the set amount of time in which you observe signs and the area or territory where you notice and become aware of them. Depending on the area or territory you choose for the oracle, you may encounter many signs or just a few.

Intuitive Awareness

As you cast the oracle stay in present time as much as possible. When you first begin, you may not always feel confident discerning signs and messages from everyday activity. This is normal. Be mindful and if you find yourself overthinking or you begin to have distracting thoughts, focus on your breath. Stay present in your body and observe what is happening around you. We often become aware of signs and messages through spontaneous intuitive awareness, feelings of heart expansion, or a gut knowing or other physical sensations. Trust it when you feel that you have encountered a sign. The *ahhh* or uplifting feeling that comes when your spirit recognizes something of value and meaning will also alert you to signs and messages. There will likely also be things, activities, people, or objects that you encounter that will have personal significance to you or trigger meaningful memories. These are also indicators of the presence of a sign.

Synchronicities

Commonly defined as an unlikely coincidence, be alert to synchronicities. Frequent synchronicities in the Living Oracle include the presence of repeating or significant numbers and colors. For instance, seeing a red car may not be a sign, but seeing three red cars one after another may be.

Numbers on license plates, buildings, street signs, and other types of signs can confirm the presence of a sign or message. Pay attention to numbers that have a personal meaning for you. For instance, encountering a building whose address has the year of your birth included in it may be a sign.

Synchronicities also include activities, objects, or things that are personal and meaningful. This might include such things as hearing a favorite song, finding a feather or coins, or encountering something that you have been thinking about or has been on your mind. For instance, spotting clowns at a children's backyard birthday party soon after sharing a childhood memory with a friend that involved a clown is likely a sign.

If you feel that something is a sign, it probably is. Don't overthink it and inwardly debate its potential significance. Accept it and document it by writing it down or recording it and move on.

Trust that the signs you receive are in your best interest and will provide you with the guidance that you most need.

INTERPRETING SIGNS

In the last section of the book there is a sign glossary that includes most of the common signs you are likely to encounter while doing the oracles outlined in this book. Because the oracles are cast in urban and residential areas and outdoors, the signs in the glossary are ones that you will find in these environments.

The sign interpretations have been given to me by my spirit helpers, intuitive insight, and my study of universal symbology. If you have a different interpretation for a sign you encounter, use what feels right for you. You may associate certain signs with memories or have a connection to specific numbers, colors, objects, or natural occurrences. Trust your first impression, your intuition, and inner knowing. The interpretations of signs in the glossary are meant to be guides and are fluid and adjustable to personal experience.

If you cannot find a sign that you encounter in the glossary and you are at loss as to its meaning, consider its characteristics and symbolic significance and how this may correlate or describe aspects of your current experience or conditions.

For instance, imagine that you encounter a single shoe on the street and you believe that this may be a sign. Symbolically, a shoe can represent walking, the feet, or being grounded. Because there is only one shoe, this may symbolically represent that someone or something is being left behind, or being alone. Maybe the shoe that you encounter is a dance shoe. This may represent movement, having fun, or joy.

Think about the current conditions in your life. Ask yourself if there is a question or concern you have been mulling over or a choice that you need to make. Make an association to the symbols. Are you grounded? Are you having fun and enjoying life? Are you feeling alone or does if feel as if there is something missing in your life?

Listen to your intuition and come up with some possible meanings. Perhaps the one dance shoe is a sign that moving forward in a relationship or new project or job will bring more joy into your life. If you are feeling left out or alone, perhaps the shoe is a sign of a romantic partner coming into your life. Listen to your gut inner knowing and your heart and the interpretation that feels right for you.

———

Now it is time to enter into the Living Oracle. Read through the different oracles and divination methods and choose what feels right for you. This is a process you can practice over and over again. The more you work with the oracles, the more natural and intuitive they will begin to flow for you.

CHAPTER 7

CASTING METHODS

The following Living Oracle rituals provide you with a few different options for invoking and eliciting sacred signs and messages. Although all of them will provide you with beneficial guidance and direction, you can choose the best one for you based on your available time, circumstances, urgency, and the type of guidance you desire.

A few of these oracles were created from ancient rituals and practices. Although they have been adapted for the Living Oracle, their timeless energy of strength and wisdom still supports and guides them.

The following three oracles generate and utilize a specific number of signs.

SIGN SIGNATURE

Do you sometimes wonder who or what may be sending you a sign or who is behind the waves of love, warmth, and comfort you are experiencing? Do you ever want to connect with a loved one on the other side or an angel or guide, but are just not sure who is close and when they are near? With this oracle exercise you can invoke the presence of a specific spirit being and form a stronger, more reliable bond.

Use the Sign Signature to ask for an identifying sign from a loved one on the other side, an ascended master, an angel, an archangel, a spirit guide, or a nature spirit. This is their signature sign and they will use it to let you know when they are present.

The Sign Signature can be practiced as often as you like; however, focus on invoking a sign from only one spirit being at a time.

Altar

Find a spot in your home, office, or outdoors that is tucked away from traffic and noise and devise a simple altar. It can be as uncomplicated as a shelf on the top of a cabinet or a circle of stones in your backyard or a natural area. Place a piece of fabric in this spot. On the fabric place any objects or photos that represent or are connected to whom you would like to contact. If you want to connect with a loved one who is one the other side you can use their photo or a personal item. To invoke a spirit guide, your higher self, angel, archangel, or ascended master, you can use a picture, pendant, crystal, gemstone, seashells, or flowers associated with the spirit being. It is also helpful to write the name of whom you would like to invoke on a piece of paper and place it on the altar. If you do not have a specific name, you can write down, "my angel," "my spirit guide," or "my higher self." Light a white candle and place it in or near the altar.

Breathe a few deep, clearing breaths and imagine white light energy completely surrounding you. Ask for the presence of whom you would like to contact to come close.

You can say something like this:

Mother Father Divine, surround me with the white light of your love and protection.

I ask for the presence of [name], loved one in spirit, my angel [or other spirit being or presence] to come close and bless me with a sign that you are near.

Repeat this or another invocation a few times. Meditate and send love and gratitude for the fulfillment of your request.

Once you have sent the message and spent a few minutes focused on the presence of whom you would like to connect with, you have completed the oracle casting. You can either leave your altar as is or wrap the objects and photos in the fabric.

Types of Signature Signs

The next step in this oracle is to be alert and patient. You may quickly become aware of a sign or it may take some time to appear. Go about your normal routines, staying alert and aware of the appearance of a sign. Try not to have an expectation as it can come to you at anytime and any place.

Common signature signs include items such as: a bird, butterfly, dragonfly, flower, gemstone, and stones and coins. Some signs are less tangible. These include such things as repeatedly hearing a favorite song or hearing soothing music, wind chimes, or your name being called. Smelling tobacco, a favorite perfume or the scent of flowers, or feeling a sudden and unexpected cool or warm breeze that is not in synch with the current weather are also common. A signature sign can also be the sensation of being touched or embraced, the flashing of lights, clocks that stop and start, phones ringing with no one on the line, or televisions or computers acting oddly.

You may receive more than one sign. This is not unusual. Sometimes the spirit realm overdoes it a bit just to make sure that we are paying attention. When you encounter what you believe to be a sign, send gratitude as an acknowledgment.

It is likely that once you identify a sign and acknowledge it, it will reappear from time to time. Each time you become aware of it, be alert to the presence of other signs. Review what is happening in your life and listen and be open to receiving guidance and direction. It might be that a loved one on the other side or a spiritual presence is seeking to assist you, or it may be simply a sign of their presence and continued love and protection.

SIGN SIGNATURE INTERPRETED

The Sign Signature is straightforward: The sign you receive is the calling card of a spirit being and does not need any further interpretation. It will continually reappear as a sign of their presence. Over time you will likely begin to gain more meaning and guidance from this sign as it becomes an energetic portal through which you can receive messages and form a stronger connection to the spirit realm.

Heather, a twenty-five-year-old graduate student, was excited to cast the Sign Signature oracle. Her mother passed over to the other side when Heather was just sixteen and she often thought her mother was close, but she was not sure. She felt this oracle might help her feel closer to her mother and be better able to detect when she was near.

While driving to the store soon after reaching out to her mother through the Sign Signature ritual, Heather encountered ducks crossing the road. While she waited for the ducks to waddle past her, she felt that this was more than a coincidence. When Heather was young her family lived in the country and had a pond in their backyard. One summer her mother surprised her with some ducklings. As the ducks crossed her path, she recalled the laughter and joy that the ducks brought her and her mother over the years. Later that afternoon when walking into the store she spotted a bright yellow t-shirt imprinted with an image of a duck with its wings spread open and a happy look on its face. She bought the shirt, knowing that with her mother's light-hearted humor, ducks were her signature sign.

TEMPLE OF SPIRIT

At times you may want to invoke just one sign for guidance, comfort, or connection with a higher power and presence. The Temple of Spirit is a one-sign oracle. It is reminiscent of the ancient oracle temples of Greece who were devoted to the Mother Goddess. The goddess was said to speak through the oracle, giving direction and guidance to those who had waited in long lines to enter the temple.

In the Temple of Spirit exercise there is no predetermined amount of time for the casting of the oracle. It begins when you make the request and ends when you receive a sign. Similar to the other exercises, begin by becoming aware of the area of concern or question that you would like addressed. Keep it simple and open-ended. Do not ask for a *yes* or *no* answer. With a one-sign oracle, a more direct request will invoke a more clear response. You can also cast this oracle for general guidance or to deepen your connection with the goddess or a higher power.

Similar to the Sign Signature oracle, it can be helpful to create a small altar indoors or outside to help you focus your intent and request. Place on the altar any objects or pictures that represent a higher loving presence or the goddess. You might also want to place flowers or a candle on the altar. With an open-hearted request for assistance, send a loving and thoughtful message into the spirit realm. Let go of your expectations and ask for guidance that is in your highest good.

When you feel as if your request is complete, send gratitude for the guidance soon to come your way and gather the altar.

After you have completed the request, be aware and alert to the emergence of a sign or message. Go about your normal routines, being mindful of the presence of a sign. Although you may not be completely certain when and if what you perceive is a sign, trust your first impression.

TEMPLE OF SPIRIT INTERPRETED

You may quickly understand the sign that you receive in the Temple of Spirit oracle. In an *ahhh* moment of understanding and intuitive insight it might make perfect sense. However, it might not. You may need some help to further interpret it. If this is true for you, consult the glossary for additional insight. If the glossary interpretation does not seem to make sense, interpret your concern, question, and current situation symbolically and look at how the meaning of the sign describes or connects to it.

For instance, Rita cast the Temple of Spirit for financial guidance. Although she worked full-time and had a well-paying job, she found that she often worried about her financial future and was concerned about the "what *ifs*." What *if* she got laid off, or what *if* an unexpected expense came her way. These doubts and fears seemed to creep up out of nowhere, causing stress and worry.

Soon after casting the Temple of Spirit, Rita encountered people dancing at an outdoor concert while on her way to visit a friend. Although she felt that this was her sign, she was unsure how to interpret it.

Looking up the glossary definition of dancing, she read: Encountering people dancing is a sign to loosen up and release stress and tension in the body and feel joy. You do not need to dance, but do something that brings you pleasure. Dancing can also be a message to allow your spirit and heart to lead you. If you have been holding back or approaching life in a more logical and rational way, people dancing is a suggestion to let go, feel the joy of life, and trust your heart.

When Rita read this interpretation she realized that her attitude about finances and money was far from joyful and free. She became aware that for her, finances symbolically represented safety and security. She believed she had to be vigilant and watch every penny and guard against loss. She realized that the sign of people dancing was a message for her to lighten up and feel more of the joy in life. In her heart she knew that she would always have enough and that enjoying her abundance would attract more of it.

SIGN MEDICINE WHEEL ORACLE

The Sign Medicine Wheel has its roots in the Native American practice of placing stones in a circular pattern to honor the four directions: north, south, east, and west. This practice is a healing rite that promotes peace and harmony among all living beings.

In the Sign Medicine Wheel, the oracle is cast to receive guidance from the four directions. There are two ways that the Sign Medicine Wheel can be cast. The first method does not require a specific area of concern or question. Each of the four directions represents and is symbolic of a specific area of your life. If you have an area, condition, concern, or question that you would like to be addressed, use the second method. In this method the four directions address the different aspects of your concern.

Although traditional medicine wheels are often located in rural areas, this oracle should be cast in an urban or residential area. Remember to have a voice recorder or journal and something to write with to record the signs.

Bring a compass to an outdoor location (many phones now come with a compass)—a street, park, parking lot, or similar area works well. Go to a spot that feels right, stand there, and send a heartfelt request for the presence of a higher power to bless you with guiding signs. Send gratitude for the messages coming your way.

The Sign Medicine Wheel yields spontaneous signs and messages. In some of the other oracle casting exercises you may have to discern signs from everyday activity. In this oracle, whatever you first encounter and feel a connection with is your sign.

With your compass, turn to the north. Notice what draws your attention. This is your sign. Write it down or voice record it. Once you have documented your sign from the north, turn to face the east. Write down the sign that you receive from the east and turn to the south, document the first sign you notice, and turn to the west and document this sign.

Send a message of gratitude. The casting is complete.

SIGN MEDICINE WHEEL ORACLE INTERPRETED

The Sign Medicine Wheel oracle yields four signs, one for each of the four directions. In this oracle you cast and then interpret it through a specific format. The first sign you encounter is the north, sign 1, the south is sign 2, the west is sign 3, and the east is sign 4.

Sign Medicine Wheel for Overall Guidance

Here is a guide for what each direction represents.

NORTH: PRACTICAL MATTERS

Represents finances, current needs and material concerns, and the current physical situation.

SOUTH: CAREER AND CREATIVITY

Represents what you are creating within your job, career, school, aspirations, and potential.

WEST: LOVE AND RELATIONSHIPS

Includes feelings and relationship with your partner, friends, family, and your connection with others.

EAST: NEW BEGINNINGS, GROWTH, AND FUTURE

Represents what may soon manifest or what is coming your way and the areas of your life where you may experience increase or growth. Allow the east sign to influence the interpretation of the other signs.

Example: Grace cast the Sign Medicine Wheel oracle for general guidance and did not have a specific question or concern in mind. Here are the signs that she received and their interpretation.

North: Practical Matters and Finances

Grace: *I saw a large red truck pulling around the back of a building.*

Glossary definition: Trucks represent service to others, strength, responsibilities, the ability to work hard or that there is work to be done. This may be in the area of your spiritual, mental, physical, or emotional health and well-being. If you stay focused you can make significant progress Trucks can be an omen of coming abundance and also symbolize your career path.

The color red can be a message of empowerment and assertiveness or a warning to subdue your anger or passion. It might also be a message to stop and assess where you are going before going any further.

Interpretation: A red truck in the north may indicate that there has been or is currently a focus on work and accomplishment in practical matters and finances. Although this is a strong and solid sign, it might be necessary to slow down and review how money is being spent and future plans.

South: Career and Creativity

Grace: *I saw large berries on a plant, I am not sure what kind. They were green and not ripe.*

Glossary definition: Encountering berries on a vine is a message of abundance, prosperity, and plans coming to fruition. Green, unripe berries are a sign to wait and be patient; a positive outcome is on the way.

Interpretation: Recent ideas and efforts related to career will soon come to fruition and be recognized.

West: Love and Relationships

Grace: *A long path, the one I had been walking on.*

Glossary definition: A walking path is a message that to make progress toward your desires and goals you need solitude and to listen within. A path in the woods or through trees and vegetation is a sign of entering into the unknown and inner mystery of self. This journey can only be undertaken solo. You may need to go it alone, at least for a while.

Interpretation: If you are in a relationship it is necessary to focus on yourself and your inner growth for the time being. As you understand and love yourself you are more able to give of yourself and be there for others. If you are single, embrace your aloneness: You are in the midst of discovering and developing your inner richness and reclaiming your authentic self.

East: New Beginnings, Future, Growth

Grace: *I saw a light blue pickup truck.*

Glossary definition: A pickup truck is a message to get to work on those things that are most meaningful and important to you. If you have been supporting others' dreams and goals, it is time to focus on you.

The color blue is a sign of peace, truth, and tranquility. Darker blues may indicate depression or feeling down. Light blues can be a message of hopeful new beginnings, new life, or a fresh start.

Interpretation: The solitary and hardworking path that Grace is on is leading to a renewed sense of self and individuality. She has every reason to feel positive and hopeful for what is coming her way.

Alternative Four Direction Oracle

If you did the Sign Medicine Wheel oracle for guidance on a specific question or area of concern, here is an alternate divination method and meaning for the four directions.

NORTH: CURRENT ISSUE

Provides insight into the present situation or condition. This often reveals what is underlying the appearances.

SOUTH: POSITIVE POTENTIAL

Reveals positive influences that may be hidden or unknown and what to put more energy and effort into.

WEST: CHALLENGES

Describes influences and conditions that may require attention and effort. This may also indicate a lesson that you need to learn.

EAST: OUTCOME

Reveals what may manifest from the current conditions.

Cast and Interpreted Four Direction Oracle

Liza cast the Sign Medicine Wheel oracle for guidance on a specific issue. Here is her question and the interpretation of the oracle.

Liza: *I strongly considering going to a writer's retreat for the first week of September. Is this a good idea? What will I gain from it if I go?*

North: Current Issue

Liza: *My sign for the north was a tall, old tree that looked huge and regal. No breeze, it was very still, almost like a painting.*

Glossary definition: A single tree represents a single individual or situation. A healthy tree with full foliage is a positive sign of good health, strength, and may be a message to claim your inner power and stand tall and be you.

Glossary definition: A clear sky with no breeze is a sign of inner clarity, wisdom, and a clear mind. It can be a message to trust your intuition and ideas—you are a clear channel for deeper awareness to surface.

Interpretation: The current issue behind the question of whether to go to the retreat is Liza's need to perceive her true self with clarity and tap into her inner wisdom.

South: Positive Potential

Liza: *I saw two guys exercising. One ran up the hill to benches, as the other ran down. They kept alternating; one ran up as the other ran down.*

Glossary definition: If people are running or jogging in opposite directions it may be a sign of an inner conflict. If you seem to be confused or not sure of what you want, look deeper, there may be unacknowledged feelings or desires. If two or more people are running together this may be a sign of cooperation and working with others toward a common goal.

Interpretation: As these runners were practicing running drills together this may indicate that the workshop will provide a supportive group environment.

East: Challenges

Liza: *I saw large white clouds from the horizon up to the sky above my head. In front of the clouds was a grey cloud bank, not clearly defined. The gray clouds reminded me of the clouds that I often saw at the beach.*

Glossary definition: White, fluffy, large clouds are a sign of peace, serenity, and spiritual insight. It may be a message to contemplate, meditate, and listen to your innermost truth. The angels are talking to you.

Grey clouds can indicate mental chatter, doubt, or confusion.

Interpretation: The white fluffy clouds indicate that if Liza is able to quiet her doubting mind, she will experience spiritual insight and attain a deep, reflective state. The challenge will be to not allow herself to become confused by the chattering mind.

The clouds stimulated Liza's memory of the beach. This may be a message to relax and adopt a leisurely approach to the workshop as these are the feelings that she most experiences while at the beach.

West: Outcome

Liza: *My sign for the west direction is a jet trail (there's no jet in the sky) that intersected the blue sky like a clearly drawn white line. It ran right down between two treetops.*

Glossary definition: Seeing a white, long, straight-line jet trail is a sign of spiritual activity and an affirmation from the spirit realm that you are being guided and led.

The oracle indicates that the spirit realm is guiding Liza to participate in the workshop. With the support of the other participants she has the opportunity to quiet her mind and access her higher self and inner voice. This will empower her to write from an inner place of authenticity.

CHAPTER 8

ADVANCED CASTING METHODS

At the heart of the Living Oracle is the communion between yourself and a higher power and presence and a strengthening of this relationship. The oracles in this chapter empower you to perceive the transcendental magic within the everyday and mundane. They are an invitation to deepen your communication and bond with higher guidance.

Unlike the oracles in the previous chapter, these oracles do not generate a specific number of signs and messages. You may receive many signs and messages or just a few. This enables you to receive more in-depth and specific guidance and direction.

In the next chapter there are several divination methods through which you can better discern and interpret the following oracles.

SIGN WALKABOUT

A Sign Walkabout is an oracle through which you invoke signs, messages, and synchronicities within a specific amount of time while walking. In many ways, the Sign Walkabout is the oracle of choice for seeking guidance and direction. It provides a natural flow for the emergence of signs and readily yields a plentiful diversity of them.

This exercise is loosely based on the Australian Aborigines walkabout. A walkabout was a right of passage for adolescent Aborigine boys who were sent alone into the wilderness for a specific amount of

time. While in this open terrain they traced the paths of their ancestors and imitated their heroic deeds.

During the Sign Walkabout you walk and wander with no predetermined destination or route, aware and attentive to the activity and
things that draw your attention. It is best to walk in an urban area,
city, or suburban or residential neighborhood. Guidance and direction is symbolically provided through the signs that you encounter
and notice.

Preparation

Before you embark on the walkabout, focus on an area in your life or
a question that you would like to receive guidance and direction
about. This can be in the area of relationships, finances, career, spirituality, life purpose, or any prominent and current issue or decision.
The question should be open-ended, not a *yes* or *no* question. However, if you do not have a current issue or specific question to focus
on, you can ask for signs, messages, and synchronicities to guide you
to your highest good.

Once you have settled on the purpose of the walkabout, ask for the
love and assistance of a higher power and wisdom to assist and guide
you in your journey. You do not have to name a particular spirit guide,
angel, or loved one. I have found that it varies from situation to situation of who comes to our aid and is the most helpful. This is usually
best worked out in the spirit realm. Simply send a message of love and
ask for the benevolence, grace, and guidance of divine wisdom, love,
and power.

Time and Place

You can predetermine a time or date or be more spontaneous and
begin the walkabout when you feel ready. Before you begin, set a time
limit for how long you will walk. It is important to have a beginning
and an end time. Although this is purely an individual preference, I
would suggest a minimum of twenty minutes and a maximum of two
hours. It is best to do the walkabout during the time of day that you
are the most alert and energized. For some this is the early morning

and for others it is the evening. However, it is best not to do the walk-about if it is dark, unless there are streetlights that enable you to clearly see what is around. Be well-rested and relaxed when you begin.

Carry a watch or some other timekeeping device. You may want to take water, a compass, a handheld or phone voice recorder, or a journal and something to write with, and wear good walking shoes.

Allow yourself some time after you have completed the walkabout to process and contemplate your experience.

Route

Although the walkabout can be done in a many different areas, it is best to walk in an area where you will encounter a variety of activities, things, and stimulation. If you do the walkabout in a familiar area, take a route that you are unfamiliar with. Do not have a destination in mind when you begin.

The walkabout begins as soon as you step outside the door of your home or, if you have driven to a location, as soon as you exit your car door. Take note of the time that you begin and if possible set the timer on your watch to the amount of time that you plan to engage in the walkabout.

The beginning of the walkabout can reveal important signs and messages and set the tone of the walkabout. Before you begin to walk, take a long, deep breath, relax, and scan your environment. Notice any-thing that draws your attention. Take your time and become aware of what provokes an inner reaction or feeling and any object, activities, or natural occurrences that you are drawn to. Write these things down in your journal or record them on your voice recorder.

The Walk

As you begin to walk, focus on your out-breath; breathe naturally and normally. Walk at a comfortable and leisurely pace. Scan the environment, taking note of what catches your attention, invokes an inner response, or triggers feelings or memories. With a relaxed gaze, stay in the present moment and allow the environment to communicate to you. Let go of your expectations of what may be significant and open your heart and mind to all that you encounter. Everything that you see may contain guidance or meaning. You will be drawn to those things that may seem to reach out to you or cause an inner physical or emotional sensation or reaction. In addition, notice any patterns that emerge. For instance, a series of cars with dented fenders or a number or color that continually reappears.

Not only are natural and man-made objects and things used as signs and messages, but sounds, the weather, overheard conversations, and other people can also be signs. Although it is best not to engage in conversation during the walkabout, if someone approaches you and wants to talk, pay attention. Many times signs and messages come through others.

Document what captures your attention and feels like a potential sign or message in your journal or on your voice recorder. Notice the feelings and thoughts that surface, but do not attach to them. Do not try to interpret or come to any conclusion as to the meaning or significance of anything that you encounter. Simply document it and stay in the present moment.

If you find yourself overthinking, or if your mind is racing and focused on daily concerns, go back to focusing on your breathing.

Continue to walk without a destination in mind. Allow your intuition to guide you and go where you feel led. Keep walking, focusing on your out-breath, and paying attention to your environment. Stay in the present moment with a receptive mind and open heart.

When the allotted time for your walk is completed, pause, scan the environment, and take note of anything that feels or seems significant. The end of the walk often yields signs and messages of special importance. Document what you perceive and any activity, objects, things, or anything else that stands out.

Resist trying to understand and interpret the signs that you have received too quickly. In the next chapter there are a few different techniques to go about interpreting them.

A Bike or Car

The Walkabout can also be undertaken while riding a bike or driving a car. However, because the focus will be on watching the road, it does not allow you to be fully attentive to what is happening around you. If you do decide to drive or ride a bike, do not have a set route or destination; like the walking walkabout, go in the direction that you feel led. A voice recorder is helpful to record the signs you observe.

If you cast the oracle while driving a car or riding a bike, please use extreme caution. Be alert, as you are responsible for your safety and the safety of other vehicles and pedestrians. The author and publisher disclaim any liability for any loss or damage of any kind incurred while practicing and casting the exercises this book.

SIGN SANCTUARY

The Sign Sanctuary exercise is similar to the Walkabout. The main difference is that instead of walking to observe signs, you sit in one location and observe what is in your environment and what comes in and out of view. This exercise is for those who are unable to walk or prefer to stay in one location. Although it is best to do the Sign Sanctuary on a park bench in an urban area, it can also be practiced in your home or office by sitting on a porch or deck or looking out a window. If you practice indoors, be sure to turn off your phone, television, computer, and any other electronic equipment that might distract you.

The territory of the Sign Sanctuary extends as far as you can see and includes whatever comes into view. If you have binoculars, it is fine to use them. Have a voice recorder or something similar close by to document the signs you observe. Predetermine the amount of time that you will sit and observe the signs. I recommend a minimum of thirty minutes. Be sure that you will not be disturbed during this period of time.

If you do the Sign Sanctuary indoors, you can arrange photos or objects close by that represent those in the spirit realm from whom you wish to receive guidance. You might also want to have a candle lit during the sign casting. Similar to the Walkabout, you can ask for guidance and advice in a specific area of concern, or you can make the request for general guidance or comfort. Begin by sitting for a few moments in quiet meditation. Ask for a higher power and presence to come close with signs, messages, and synchronicities for guidance and direction. The sign casting territory in the Walkabout Oracle tends to be ripe with stimulation and activity. Because of this it may become necessary to discern signs and messages from the everyday, routine comings and goings.

Because the Sign Sanctuary exercise is more stationary, it is important to pay attention to whatever comes into your environment. Unless your Sign Sanctuary territory is a busy and active urban area, review everything that comes into view during the allotted time as a possible sign.

Document the signs and messages you observe by either writing down or recording them on a voice recorder.

SIGN VISION QUEST

The Sign Vision Quest exercise is similar to the Sign Sanctuary and Walkabout in most ways. The difference is in the territory and amount of time devoted to observing signs and messages. During the Sign Sanctuary and Walkabout, you sit or walk for a specific amount of time; the Vision Quest exercise can last a few days or more.

The Sign Vision Quest is suggestive of the Native American Vision Quest. During a traditional Native American Vision Quest, a person spends one to four days and nights alone in nature communing with the spirit realm, nature, and the creator. During this time, the meaning of life and one's personal destiny and purpose is revealed through visions, dreams, or signs.

Begin the Sign Vision Quest by determining the amount of time devoted to casting the oracle. One to three days tends to be sufficient. Any longer and you will likely lose focus. The territory includes wherever you are during the allowed time. This might be in your home, workplace, while walking in the park, or while shopping—whatever you normally do. However, it is important to spend some time alone, listen and act on where you feel led, and get out of your routines as much as possible. It can be helpful to decrease and limit your exposure to television, the Internet, social media, and phone and texting during this time.

As in all of the oracle exercises, determine the area of your life where you would like to receive guidance and direction. If you do not have a specific concern you can cast the oracle for general guidance, comfort, or connection with the spirit realm. You can also follow the path of the traditional Vision Quest and ask for increased self-awareness of your purpose and destiny.

Start the casting with a request for the guiding benevolence of a higher power. Once you do this, take a few moments to scan your environment, paying attention to anything that draws your attention or seems to speak to you.

During the time of the casting, go about your day-to-day activities, taking note of what seems to speak to you and gets your attention. Maintain a heightened sense of awareness, being alert to what feels to be a sign or message. The challenge is to stay alert and mindful of the process and the unfolding of the oracle. Remember to write down or record the sign or message as soon as you receive it.

Unlike the other exercises, in the Sign Vision Quest, signs and messages may surface through your dreams. If you remember a dream during the allotted time that you are casting the oracle, record any significant signs and messages that you receive from the dream. Pay particular attention to any synchronicities in the dream that may be connected to signs or messages that you receive while awake. It is fine if you do not dream or if the dream does not seem to contain a clear sign or message. It is not essential for this exercise. Any signs that you receive during waking hours will work.

The Sign Walkabout, the Sign Vision Quest, and the Sign Sanctuary oracles will each yield a varying number of signs. At times you may receive many clear and easily noticeable signs and at other times you may have difficulty discerning a few. There is no set amount of signs that you should receive when you cast these oracles.

CHAPTER 9

DIVINATION METHODS

If you have cast the Sign Walkabout, Sign Vision Quest, or the Sign Sanctuary oracles, there are several different divination methods through which you can interpret and gain insight and a more complete understanding of your oracle.

Similar to tarot card spreads, oracle divination methods provide you with a format to further discern and gain deeper understanding from your signs. After reading over the different divination methods, choose the one that best addresses your concern or issue.

If you receive more signs than the divination method requires, or you are not sure of the placement of each sign, there is an exercise at the end of this chapter to guide you in determining the signs to use and their placement within the divination method of your choosing.

THREE SIGN GUIDANCE

The Three Sign Guidance method can be used for many common issues such as finance and career, or for more specific personal issues. It brings clarity to confusing circumstances and helps you to have a better grasp of how to resolve or move on from a perplexing situation.

Sign 1: Situation

Helps to clarify the conditions that you are currently experiencing and what may be hidden.

Sign 2: Challenge
Defines the inherent lesson within the situation or what you may need to focus on and confront within the current situation.

Sign 3: Guidance
Provides direction and possibilities for the current issue.

ALTERNATIVE THREE SIGN GUIDANCE
This method provides insight into a current situation or issue and shows how it has progressed and its possible outcome.

Sign 1: Past
This sign expresses what has led to the current situation or issue; where you are coming from.

Sign 2: Present
Illustrates the current condition and what you may not be aware of; what is behind the appearances.

Sign 3: Future
Describes what is coming and how the current issue or situation may evolve.

FOUR SIGN LIFE PURPOSE
This method is best used if you cast the oracle to better understand your pupose or destiny.

Sign 1: Your Connection to Your Life's Purpose
This sign will help you to recognize if you are in sync with your overall purpose or if you are struggling against it.

Sign 2: Purpose with Other Relationships; Family, Friends
Provides you with insight into your purpose with others, and your relationships with family and friends. What you are learning and what you are receiving. The role that you play in the lives of others.

Sign 3: Purpose in the World: Community, Service
Sheds light on your purpose with issues and concerns that affect the larger community and your gift to the world.

Sign 4: Soul Purpose, Evolution, Lessons
Reveals what your soul has come here to express, learn, and give to others.

FIVE SIGN GUIDANCE

This divinition method is a good one to use to gain deeper insight into your question or area of concern. It covers a wide range of areas and topics.

Sign 1: Your Concern or Issue
Describes influences related to the current question.

Sign 2: The Unconscious and Unknown
Reveals unconscious influences affecting the concern.

Sign 3: Advice
Provides guidance as to how to proceed.

Sign 4: What Is Coming, the Near Future
This sign gives insight into what may soon manifest.

Sign 5: Overview Unifying Sign
The Overview and Unifying Sign is the most influential sign in this oracle.

SIX SIGN RELATIONSHIP GUIDANCE

If your questions have to do with a relationship, use this divination method.

Sign 1: You
Describes your hopes, expectations, feelings, and attitudes.

Sign 2: The Other

Reveals the other person's hopes, expectations, feelings, and attitudes.

Sign 3: Connection

Provides insight into what has brought you both together.

Sign 4: Strengths

Reveals the positive potential of the relationship.

Sign 5: Challenges

What you may need to work on and issues to be addressed.

Sign 6: Potential for Long-Term Future

This sign influences the other signs.

SIX SIGN SPIRIT DIVINATION

This divination method allows spirit beings to communicate with and guide you. Use it if you cast the oracle to receive guidance from the spirit realm or a specific spirit being, angel, spirit guide, or loved one.

Sign 1: Where You Are Now

This first sign describes the issue that the sprit realm would like to address and where they perceive you to be at this time.

Sign 2: Your Next Step or Lesson

Reveals your next step or lesson in consciousness development.

Sign 3: Challenges

Helps you become aware of what you may externally or internally need to confront.

Sign 4: Strengths: What You Have Mastered

Illustrates what you have already learned and what you can now draw from.

Sign 5: Guidance

Suggestions and advice from your higher self and the spirit realm; may involve a choice or further effort on your part.

Sign 6: Outcome, Future

Reveals what may manifest from the actions and lessons that you are currently learning.

The following chapter illustrates examples of oracles that have been interpreted through these different divination methods.

SIGN DETERMINER AND PLACEMENT EXERCISE

The number of signs that you receive through these oracles are random. Because of this you may receive more signs than the divination method calls for. When you have more signs than you need or if you want to better discern the placement of the signs, use the following system before interpreting them.

Begin by cutting up small strips of paper in the same amount of signs that you have received. Write down one sign on each slip of paper. One sign on one strip of paper.

When you have written down all the signs, turn the strips of paper over on a flat surface so you cannot see what is written on them.

Choose your divination method and the number of signs that you will need. Depending on what you choose, this may be three, four, five, or six signs.

Close your eyes and focus on the question or area of concern that you cast the oracle for. Move the palm of your hand over the strips of paper and pick up the strip of paper that you feel drawn to. This is sign one. Continue this process and pick up sign two. Continue until you have picked up the number of signs that you will need for your divination method. Place them in the order that you have picked them up.

If you use a divination method that requires the exact number of signs that you received you can use your signs in the order that you received them. The first sign is sign one, the second sign you encounter is sign two, etc. Or you can use the above method to choose their placement.

How to Work with a Double Sign

There will be times when you encounter a sign that is a combination of more than one sign.

For instance, encountering sparrows drinking from a small pond. Both the sparrows and the pond are signs and should be written down as one sign on one slip of paper. When you interpret this sign, look up the meaning of sparrows and the meaning of small pond in the glossary.

THE INTERPRETATION OF SPARROWS:
The sparrow is a sign to be industrious. Enjoy your friends and other social relationships and do not underestimate yourself. Power is in small acts of kindness. The sparrow can also bring you the message to be modest. Work toward your goals, but for the time being, allow others to take center stage.

THE INTERPRETATION OF A POND:
A tranquil pond or lake is a sign to avoid overreaching. This is not the time to make plans or focus on the future. Success will come as you stay in present time and attend to what is happening right now. A pond can also be a calming message to be still and listen within.

Then look for commonalities and connections within the signs.

Both of these symbols have to do with staying in present time, being modest, and focusing on small actions. This can also be interpreted as a message to be industrious, enjoy what is in front of you, and avoid overreaching.

Look for what stands out to you and trust your intuitive sense when interpreting a double sign as one message.

CHAPTER 10

EXAMPLES OF CAST AND INTERPRETED ORACLES

Casting and interpreting the Living Oracle is a new way to perceive yourself and the world around you, and to receive guidance. Symbolically interpreting the everyday and common things and activities that you regularly encounter shifts your perception and assumptions. As you perceive the spiritual magic hidden and encoded within, new insights are revealed and your connection with the unseen realms of wisdom and love becomes stronger.

While developing the Living Oracle I was fortunate to have friends and clients willing to enthusiastically jump in and experience this unique system for themselves. This chapter includes examples of some of their interpreted oracles. Reading through them will give you a sense of how to approach and symbolically interpret your signs within the divination methods.

It may take some practice and trust in your intuitive insights and feelings to become fully comfortable interpreting sacred signs, messages, and synchronicities. Most of the common signs that you may receive are listed in the glossary. Reading their symbolic interpretation will help you to better understand and interpret them. If you have a different interpretation or association, or if you have an intuitive sense of what a sign or message personally means to you, go with your interpretation. If the sign or message that you encounter while casting the oracle is not in the glossary, use your intuition or symbolic association to interpret the sign. Be flexible in your approach to interpretation and allow yourself to be guided throughout the process.

HOW TO APPROACH SIGN PLACEMENT

It is important to note that when working with certain divination methods, a sign may not seem to make sense within the context of its placement.

For instance: Let's say that you cast the oracle to receive guidance and direction on whether or not to leave your current job. You choose the three-sign divination method to interpret your signs. In this method the first sign represents the past, the second sign represents the present, and the third sign represents the future.

Perhaps your second sign is a dented and scratched car. Given that your question involves a career decision, the dented car may not seem to make sense to you. The second sign placement symbolizes the current condition and what you may not be aware of or what is behind the appearances. If this happens and it likely will, look up the glossary interpretation of your sign. Then perceive the events of your life symbolically and draw associations between this and the sign or message that you received.

The glossary interpretation of a dented car:

A car with dents and scratches or in need of bodywork may be a sign of difficulties and the stress and strain that it has had on you. It can also be a sign of a wounded ego and feeling picked on or a message to pay attention to how you are treating others.

While initially this may not appear to provide you with guidance on your question about your career, look at the events of your life through a symbolic lens.

For instance: Ask yourself if you feel like this dented car in any way. Have you been feeling pushed or not respected in your current job? Are you reacting from your ego in wanting to leave and go to another company?

Symbolically interpret the glossary definition in the broadest way possible. Look for connections in your present experiences and conditions. Signs are often the jumping-off point to becoming more aware of other factors and influences as well as feelings, thoughts, and unconscious drives that may be affecting your question or present conditions.

Three Sign Guidance Divination

Nora cast the Sign Walkabout oracle. Instead of walking, she decided to ride her bike on a bike path on the outskirts of a city. Married for a little over two years, she was contemplating having children. Her husband was undecided about becoming a father and he wanted Nora to be sure that she wanted to be a mom before becoming pregnant. She cast the oracle to become more clear and gain insight and guidance on this big decision. She received three signs within the thirty-minute casting time period.

Sign 1: Current Situation—Recycling Truck
Sign 2: Challenge—A Butterfly
Sign 3: Guidance—A Crew Working on the Sewer

Interpretation

SIGN 1: CURRENT SITUATION—RECYCLING TRUCK
Glossary definiton: A recycling truck is a message to accept all of who you are. If you are feeling guilt or a lack of self-worth for past actions or experiences, forgive yourself. Learn from the lessons that life has sent your way and use this wisdom and awareness to create more of what you desire.

This message had a profound effect on Nora. When she read it, she acknowledged that motherhood was highly prized by her family. It was always assumed that she would have a baby. She felt guilty and wondered if something was wrong with her for focusing more on her career than on creating a family. This sign helped her to realize that she had to accept her feelings about her personal desire to be a mother and not judge herself.

SIGN 2: CHALLENGE—BUTTERFLY
Glossary definiton: A butterfly is a positive sign that a loved one on the other side or an angel is with you. Butterflies can also be a sign of

transformation and the emergence of your true self after difficulties or healing and renewed health after illness.

The second sign represents challenge. While it may not appear that a butterfly can indicate an issue to be overcome and worked through, for Nora, her challenge was to allow herself to transform and let her true desires emerge. The butterfly inspired and gave her hope that an angel was watching over this process as she grappled with this important decision.

SIGN 3: GUIDANCE—CREW WORKING ON THE SEWER

Glossary definiton: Work being done underground or in a sewer or subway is a sign that something in the past or something you have left behind needs to be revisited. The past holds the key to understanding and moving forward in the future.

As Nora contemplated the message of this sign, she remembered how from a young age she had always wanted to care for wounded, ill, and lost animals. Although she rescued dogs and volunteered at an animal shelter, she wanted to do more. She realized that, for now, animals were her passion and in her heart she had always wanted to go to veterinary school. She had thought that she was being selfish by not focusing on creating more of a family. However, she now realized that before she became a mother she wanted to explore this goal.

ALTERNATIVE THREE SIGN GUIDANCE

Eric cast the Sign Walkabout oracle and decided to interpret it with the Three Sign Guidance method. Although he was satisfied with his current job, he had recently been contacted by a job recruiter about an open position in an area that he was interested in exploring. He did not know whether to pursue the new position and decided to cast the oracle for guidance. He received a total of six signs. After writing them all down on slips of paper, he picked out the three signs needed for this divination method. They were a car repair shop, a magnolia tree, and a bookstore, in this order.

Sign 1: Past—Car Repair Shop
Sign 2: Present—Magnolia Tree
Sign 3: Future—Bookstore

Interpretation

SIGN: PAST—CAR REPAIR SHOP

Glossary definiton: A car repair shop is a sign to seek guidance, advice, or insight from another, possibly a professional. This may be a message to fine-tune your skills and abilities and be at your optimum mind, body, and spirit.

This sign indicates that the current career opportunity has come to Eric from his past desire to seek out opportunities to develop and refine his skills and abilities. Advice from business associates or mentors have also influenced his desire to advance his career.

SIGN 2: PRESENT—MAGNOLIA TREE

Glossary definiton: Magnolia trees are a sign of nobility and the ability to confront obstacles with a calm and centered will and determination. Magnolia blossoms or flowers are a sign of beauty and grace, a divine kiss of kindness.

Even though Eric is satisfied in his current profession, he is most happy when he is learning new things and personally and professionally growing. This sign is a confirmation that the present opportunity may be an answer to this wish and desire, a gift and opportunity from the spirit realm.

SIGN 3: FUTURE—BOOKSTORE

Glossary definiton: A bookstore is message to explore new ideas, be creative, and welcome new possibilities into your life. You may need inspiration to get out of a rut or routine. A bookstore may also be a sign to write and may be announcing literary success.

This sign indicates that the possible job in question offers Eric the opportunity to be creative and explore new ideas. It is another confirmation that this is a good time to further his career and follow up on this opportunity.

FOUR SIGN LIFE PURPOSE GUIDANCE

With an interest in all things Native American, Jessica decided to cast the Vision Quest oracle. In keeping with the spirit of this oracle, she wanted to know more about her life purpose. Because her workplace tended to be hectic and busy, she decided to start the oracle casting on Saturday and end on Monday morning. To get the most from the oracle she did not turn on her computer or television and spent limited time on the phone during this period.

The signs that she encountered during the weekend of the Sign Vision Quest included an owl on a tree outside her bedroom window, a couple kissing in the park, a small white poodle, people going into a church, a small fountain with crows drinking from it, a mother pushing a stroller, kids riding their bikes, and a billboard advertising an insurance company with the words, "You Are in Good Hands." Jessica also had a dream on Sunday night that she was flying an airplane alongside a flock of geese.

After writing her signs down on slips of paper, the four signs that she picked in order were the billboard, the dream of flying the plane, kids riding bikes, and people going into church.

Sign 1: Your Connection to Your Life's Purpose—Billboard

Sign 2: Purpose with Other Relationships: Family, Friends—Dream of Flying the Plane

Sign 3: Purpose in the World: Community, Service—Kids on Bikes

Sign 4: Soul Purpose, Evolution, Lessons—Church

Use Sign 1 in relation to the other signs. It will give you insight as to the interconnection of your overall purpose.

Interpretation

SIGN 1: CONNECTION TO LIFE PURPOSE—BILLBOARD WITH THE PHRASE, "YOU ARE IN GOOD HANDS"

This billboard phrase is a clear message that Jessica is being watched over and guided. After she read the interpretation of this sign, she told me that she felt this was a sign letting her know that God was directing her purpose. As long as she listened within and trusted where she felt led, Jessica believed that she would stay on track with her higher purpose.

SIGN 2: PURPOSE WITH OTHERS: FRIENDS, FAMILY—DREAM OF FLYING IN PLANE WITH GEESE

Dreams that you have while casting the Vision Quest oracle are interpreted as a sign.

Glossary definiton: An airplane can indicate rising above current problems and issues, the need or ability to see the big picture, expansion of consciousness, taking flight, or leaving your current situation. It can also be a confirming message that you are communicating and connecting to your guides, helpers, and loved ones in the spirit realm.

Geese ask you to be sure that the path that you are on is your own. We often compromise and allow others to sway our opinions and influence our actions. Look into your heart and feel what is true for you. A flock of geese symbolizes lifelong companionship and is a message that you are never alone; your spiritual loved ones are close.

Flying the airplane may be a sign that Jessica has the ability to help others to see beyond their challenges and difficulties and gain new insight. The flock of geese might also indicate that Jessica may be able to guide others to express their true selves and to look into their hearts. It may be that Jessica's purpose with others is to share her individuality, higher consciousness, and perceptions. She might also be able to communicate with the spirit realm and provide messages of guidance and comfort to others.

Sign 3: Purpose in the World—Kids Riding Bikes

Glossary definiton: A bicycle is a sign of balance, freedom, and personal effort. It is a message that you are in charge of where you are going and your progress in getting there. It may also be a message to be flexible and avoid extremes in work and pleasure. If you have been pushing yourself, it may be time to be take a more leisurely approach.

Glossary definiton: Children playing can be a sign of happiness and simplicity, and a message to adopt a carefree attitude. It may also be a message to reclaim an aspect of yourself from the past that may have been forgotten or left behind. This may be a personal truth, a belief in what is possible, or your innocence.

Both children and a bicycle are signs of taking a leisurely and lighthearted approach. It may be that Jessica's gift to the world manifests through purity, innocence, and in helping others to discover these qualities in themselves. She brings the gift of fun and lightheartedness to the world.

SIGN 4: SOUL PURPOSE—PEOPLE GOING INTO A CHURCH
Glossary definiton: People going in or out of a church is a message that currently or in the near future there will be an increase in spiritual activity with others or with a group.

This sign suggests that Jessica's soul purpose is to be actively engaged with others in some form of spiritual practice. This may be through a specific belief system or through a more open and fluid spirituality. This is a sign to Jessica that her soul growth and spiritual development will be best supported and enhanced through her connection to others and in her relationships.

The first sign, the billboard message, "You Are in Good Hands," influences the other three signs. In relation to her purpose with others, the billboard emphasizes that Jessica is meant to share her personal insights and possibly share divine message of guidance and love. For her purpose in the world, the billboard affirms that Jessica maintain her childlike innocence and lighthearted approach. Because of the spiritual nature of the billboard, this may further indicate that her soul purpose is to spiritually grow and connect with others and that she is being guided. Through this lens it becomes apparent that Jessica's overall purpose is to maintain a conscious connection with the divine and to be a conduit of this joy and pure presence.

FIVE SIGN DIVINATION

Emily cast the Sign Sanctuary oracle and interpreted it through the Five Sign Guidance method.

A single woman in her late fifties with grown children who no longer live at home, Emily was contemplating moving to the mountains. She had always wanted to get out of the city and live closer to nature. Yet, she felt stifled with inertia and did not know what to do. She cast the oracle for guidance and to gain clarity about this issue.

Emily received five signs when she cast the oracle whie sitting on a park bench in a city park. Her signs in the order that she received them are a red convertible, a liquor store, a mud puddle, a robin, and ants.

Sign 1: Your Concern or Issue—Red Convertible
Sign 2: The Unconscious and Unknown—Liquor Store

Sign 3: Advice—Mud Puddle

Sign 4: What Is Coming, the Near Future—Robin

Sign 5: Overview Unifying Sign—Ants

The Overview Unifying Sign is the most influential sign in this oracle. The other signs should be interpreted with this sign in mind.

Interpretation

SIGN 1: YOUR CONCERN OR ISSUE—RED CONVERTIBLE

Glossary definiton: The color red can be a message of empowerment and assertiveness or a warning to subdue your anger or passion. It may also be a sign to stop before going ahead with a project, relationship, or venture.

A convertible may be a message to free yourself from negative beliefs, judgments, and thoughts. Open your mind to higher thoughts and allow the light of spiritual wisdom to expand your consciousness. It is also a sign of freedom and enjoyment and allowing yourself to let go.

The red convertible symbolizes Emily's situation quite well. While moving offers her the freedom to create a new life, explore new options, and the joy of being in a location where she has always wanted to live, she may need to examine any beliefs and judgments that are holding her back. The color red may be a message to be assertive in taking action on what she desires.

SIGN 2: THE UNCONSCIOUS AND UNKNOWN—A LIQUOR STORE

Glossary definiton: A liquor store is a message to keep things in perspective and balance. If you are stressed and anxious, loosen up and relax. If you feel a little lost and without direction, establish step-by-step goals. It can also indicate that you or someone close to you may have a problem with alcohol.

This sign suggests that Emily may need to approach her possible move one step at a time. She may also need to become aware of any hidden tension or anxiety that may be affecting her clarity of mind and preventing her from connecting with her heart's desire. Because this sign is in the position of the unconscious, it indicates that there may be past experiences and fears that are unknowingly affecting her decision-making.

SIGN 3: ADVICE HOW TO PROCEED—MUD
Glossary definiton: Mud or muddy water is a sign of confusion, indecision, and procrastination. It is a message that even though you may not be sure of what to do or how to proceed, take some form of action. Move forward in some way, even if you are unsure, and clarity will follow.

This sign is a message to Emily to continue to investigate and explore a move. She may want to visit the location where she is considering moving and become more familiar with the community and what it has to offer. Consulting a financial advisor and real estate agent might also give her much-needed information to make a decision.

SIGN 4: WHAT IS COMING, THE NEAR FUTURE—ROBIN
Glossary definiton: A robin is a sign of joy, laughter, and new growth. Open your heart and allow the energy of renewal to revitalize you. Robins encourage you to find pleasure in the mundane.

This sign confirms that Emily is moving in the right direction. The robin is an auspicious sign foretelling that she will soon experience joy and feelings of renewal and positivity.

SIGN 5: OVERVIEW UNIFYING SIGN—ANTS
Glossary definiton: Ants are a message that hard work yields positive results. If you feel that your efforts are not seen or are disregarded, ants are a sign that this is temporary. Abundance and positive results are coming your way.

This sign influences all of the other signs. It is a message for Emily to become active and work toward her goal of moving and fulfilling a life-long desire. Sometimes taking a step back and waiting is necessary. This is not the case for Emily. It is made clear in the oracle that action is needed to accomplish this goal. Her efforts will pay off in positive and joyful ways.

Six Sign Spirit Divination

Kristi did not have a question in mind and cast the Walkabout oracle for general guidance. During an hour walk, she received many signs including a green moth on her front door; a mail truck; laundry on an outdoor clothesline; a little girl playing; a foot bridge; a large black dog; a man with a cast on his leg; wind gusts; an aggressive dog; a large fallen tree limb; road construction; a backhoe; yellow daisies; and people doing yard work.

After writing the signs down of slips of paper and folding them in half, Kristi randomly picked out six signs in this order: wind gusts, yellow daisies, yard work, clothesline with laundry, road construction, mail truck.

Sign 1: Where You Are Now—Wind Gusts
Sign 2: Your Next Step or Lesson—Yellow Daises
Sign 3: Challenges—Yard Work
Sign 4: Strengths, What You Have Mastered—Clothesline
Sign 5: Guidance—Road Construction
Sign 6: Outcome, Future—Mail Truck

Interpretation

Sign 1: Where You Are Now—Wind Gusts
Glossary definiton: Wind gusts suggest that your thinking may be scattered and you may need to focus your ideas and thoughts. Wind gusts may also be a message to pay attention to intuitive insights.

Kristi knew that her chattering mind created confusion and indecision. She would go from one thought to another and another. Although she felt that she received intuitive messages she would often overthink them and talk herself out of trusting them.

Sign 2: Your Next Step—Yellow Daisies
Glossary definiton: The daisy is symbolic of purity, innocence, patience, and simplicity. Encountering daisies is a message to draw from these qualities and let go of expectations. Something may be coming

your way or will be offered to you that might not initially seem to be what you want or what you are looking for. However, in time you will recognize this as a true gift.

The color yellow is a sign of happiness, energy, intellect, and mental stimulation. Yellow may also be a message of betrayal, deceit, and indecisiveness. Along with orange, yellow is associated with the sun.

When Kristi read the symbolic interpretation for yellow daisies, she told me that it described how she wanted to live: simply, happy, and without expectation. She felt that this sign, which represented her next step, was indicating what she was feeling, but she was having a hard time putting into words. She wanted to move forward in a more positive way in life and she felt that the yellow daises were a sign from her angels letting her know that this was possible.

SIGN 3: CHALLENGES—YARD WORK

Glossary definiton: People doing yard work, gardening, or farming is a message to take action and root out negativity and habits that are not supporting your higher aims and desires.

Along with chaotic thinking, Kristi was a constant worrier and often feared the worst. This sign helped her to become aware of how her habitual thoughts were affecting her outlook and the quality of life. She felt motivated and determined to let go and change her perspective.

SIGN 4: STRENGTHS, HOW TO PROCEED—CLOTHESLINE WITH LAUNDRY

Glossary definiton: A clothesline with laundry hanging from it is a sign of clearing the mind and emotions of any negative, judgmental, and stressful thoughts and feelings. Focusing on what may appear to be small and insignificant personality deficits and weaknesses and releasing them allows the light of your soul to shine through. A clothesline may also be a message to be honest and open and allow others to see the true you.

Kristi was surprised that the interpretation of the clothesline seemed to reinforce the previous signs and further motivated her to become more aware of the negative and stressful thoughts that she was prone to and let them go. As she contemplated this sign she became aware that she often hid her true feelings and thoughts from others. *Maybe*, she thought, *this sign is letting me know that positive things will come from letting others see the true me.*

Sign 5: Guidance—Road Construction

Glossary definiton: Encountering construction workers, working on roads or in other public places, is a sign that you may need help, guidance, and support from others to move forward in creating and fulfilling your dreams and desires. This may also be a sign to be there for others and help them to build their dreams.

For several weeks, Krista had contemplated working with a life coach. She knew that another's support would help her to move forward into the happiness that sign 2, the yellow daises, spoke of. This message gave her the push she needed.

Sign 6: Outcome, Future—Mail Truck

Glossary definiton: A mail, UPS, FedEx, or other mail or package delivery truck may be a sign that much-needed insights, information, or communication is coming your way. You may also have information or insights that others need. This may come through an intuitive or psychic gift. It might also point to your ability to intuit messages for yourself and others and communicate with the other side.

Krista found this sign to be helpful and comforting. Both of her parents had passed over and were now on the other side. She often felt their presence and hoped that they were watching over her. She also found it encouraging to know that new insights and information would emerge as she was better able to focus on the positive and trust her intuitive insights.

"Maybe as I do the inner work that the other signs are pointing to, my intuition will become stronger and I will be able to connect more clearly with my mother and father. Who knows," she said, "maybe one day I can give messages to others. I would love to do this."

Six Sign Relationship Divination

Derek met Carrie at a friend's wedding. They both felt an immediate attraction and after a night of laughter and dancing they exchanged phone numbers. In the first few months of their relationship they saw one another three or four times a week. The relationship was easy and they shared a common passion for long-distance cycling and cooking. After about six months of dating, Derek began to feel that Carrie might be too controlling and she seemed to need to have things her way most of the time. Although he still had feelings for her, he began to question if the relationship was positive for him. Confused and not sure of what to do, he cast a Sign Walkabout to gain insight and guidance. During the walkabout he encountered six signs that he used in the order that he received them: a park; safety cones; a restaurant; a small brown dog; a junk car; and a cactus.

Sign 1: Your Hopes Expectations, Feelings, and Attitudes—A Park

Sign 2: The Other's Hopes, Expectations, Feelings, and Attitudes—Safety Cones

Sign 3: Connection, What Has Brought You Both Together—Restaurant

Sign 4: Strengths, The Positive Potential of the Relationship—Small Brown Dog

Sign 5: Challenges, What You May Need to Work On and Issues to Be Addressed—Junk Car

Sign 6: Potential for Long-term Future. This sign influences the other signs—Cactus

Interpretation

SIGN 1: YOUR HOPES, EXPECTATIONS, FEELINGS, AND ATTITUDES—A PARK

Glossary definiton: A park is a message to take it easy, contemplate the simple beauty of life, and refresh your spirit. A park may also be a sign of a romantic relationship coming your way or being rekindled.

Derek felt that this sign represented his desire to be in a romantic, casual, and easygoing relationship. His hope was that Carrie felt the same way.

Sign 2: The Other's Hopes, Expectations, Feelings, and Attitudes—Safety Cones

Glossary definiton: Orange safety cones symbolize the need for you to be cautious, alert, and pay attention to details. They are a message to focus on what may appear to be minor and small issues. In this way you are able to circumvent challenges and difficulties.

When Derek read the interpretation of this sign, he realized that what we he believed to be controlling behavior by Carrie might simply be her more cautious and detail-oriented personality. She seemed to notice everything he did and he found himself frequently annoyed by this personality trait.

Derek also wondered if this sign was telling him to pay attention to his feelings about the difference between his and Carrie's personalities. Even though they were minor issues, ignoring them may not be the right thing to do.

Sign 3: Connection, What Has Brought You Both Together—Restaurant

Glossary definiton: Symbolic of the quality of your relationships with others, a restaurant is a message to evaluate the care and nurturing that you receive from friends, family, and loved ones, and to become more conscious of the nurturing and care that you provide to others.

Derek wondered how much emotional depth he and Carrie would be able to share. He knew that he was not opening his heart and giving in the way that Carrie needed him to. He also felt that he was not receiving the positive support from her that he longed for.

Sign 4: Strengths, The Positive Potential of the Relationship—Small Brown Dog

Glossary definiton: A small dog is a sign that you have within you the qualities and attributes to fulfill your purpose. Don't underestimate what you have to offer others and the world. You have a powerful and loving heart and soul.

Brown is associated with nature spirits. It is a message to connect with the earth, be practical, and trust your instincts.

Derek knew that he truly wanted a loving relationship and he knew that this was what Carrie also wanted. Part of his initial attraction to her was her strength and her deep, soulful nature. Yet, when he contemplated the signs and their interpretation, he realized that he had to trust his instincts. When he listened within, he felt that they would not be able to make the relationship work.

SIGN 5: CHALLENGES, WHAT YOU MAY NEED TO WORK ON AND ISSUES TO BE ADDRESSED—JUNK CAR

Glossary definiton: A car that has been junked or is no longer operational can indicate that a present issue or concern is not viable. If you have a question about a relationship, new career path, or new undertaking, this is a warning of heartache or disappointing outcome.

Although this sign was discouraging to Derek, he felt that something or someone really wanted him to get the message that he and Carrie may not be compatible. As much as he wanted the relationship to work the signs seemed to telling him that it might not.

SIGN 6: POTENTIAL FOR LONG-TERM FUTURE—CACTUS

This sign influences the other signs.

Glossary definiton: A cactus symbolizes emotional hurt, feeling slighted, or feeling that you have been treated unfairly. It is a message that you have the inner resources to go it alone if necessary and to heal.

When Derek read the interpretation of this sign he felt that it was a confirmation of his gut feeling and the other signs. The relationship with Carrie was not viable. Although he felt sad, he knew that the kindest thing to do was to end the relationship and at some point try to build a friendship. He was also aware that they would both in time find the soul mate that they were looking for and be able to get through the breakup.

―――――

Through these examples you can begin to get a sense of how to interpret the Living Oracle. Be flexible and listen within to the interpretation that feels right for you. If you find yourself frustrated or unsure of how to proceed, take a break and focus on something else. When the conscious-thinking mind is engaged elsewhere, your intuitive knowing will more easily surface and offer you the clarity and interpretation that you have been looking for.

CONCLUSION: GOING FORWARD, BEING LED

This morning I did my normal Monday morning routine. I woke up early and headed to the pool. On my way there I passed through several green lights with ease. Once at the pool my preferred locker, number seven, was available. Even though the pool tends to be crowded in the early morning, I was able to find an empty lane with no wait time. As I swam my first laps, I smiled. This was going to be a good day, all the signs were there.

Not every morning is like this. There are days when things do not line up quite so easily. Traffic is heavy, I hit the red lights, and there is no hot water in the showers. When I encounter these kind of signs, I know not to take things too personally and get bogged down with frustrations. This is just how the day is flowing. I might need to better pay attention to detail or perhaps check my attitude and be honest about any negativity that I may be harboring.

Through actively pursuing signs and omens, and over the course of writing this book, I have become more intimately familiar with the symbolic and metaphoric nature of everyday things and activities. Signs have become a natural part of my day-to-day life and I find myself noticing and tuning in to the messages that always seem to be present.

As you invoke signs and messages and develop your own internal code to understanding the meaning within them, you begin to freely dialogue with the world around you. What was once mundane transforms into the meaningful.

At first glance, discerning a sign from the many things and activities that you encounter on a daily basis may seem to be a guessing game. However, your intuitive muscle will eventually strengthen and you will hear, feel, know, and become aware when you encounter a sign and be able to discern its message. At times the meaning of a sign or synchronicity will be clear and you will be able to sense who has sent it to you. At other times, you may feel challenged and not sure how to penetrate the meaning hidden within the language of a sign.

Signs and messages speak to us through a code that can at times be frustrating and difficult to decipher. They break through our linear and logical way of thinking and speak to our heart and soul. Making this shift from the rational to the intuitive is not always easy. Instead of receiving clear guidance, you may at times find yourself more perplexed and confused. If this happens, I encourage you to hang in there and not give up. If you notice a sign, but are just not sure if it really is one, stop the inner back-and-forth debate and overthinking and simply accept that it is a sign and that its meaning will be revealed. Whatever you notice and gets your attention is speaking to you.

If you receive a sign and it is not included in the glossary, trust your feelings and inner sense of knowing as to its meaning. If you are not sure if you are interpreting a sign correctly, don't worry. The universe is quite repetitive. It will let you know over and over again in various creative ways if there is a message for you.

Signs change us. On a daily basis we tend to scramble about trying to get everything done and attended to. We become stressed, anxious, and unconscious of the unseen influences and support that is always available. Becoming aware of signs can be a meditation that wakes you to your connectedness with all of life and helps you to be in the present moment. As you allow your creative soul forces to empower you to better notice and decipher the meaning of signs and message, your perception of reality evolves.

We have been led to believe that the finite world of matter and material things is inert and incapable of conveying wisdom and love. However, as you work with the Living Oracle, the innate ability to notice and decipher signs and messages will rise from the depths of your soul knowing and become natural. One day you may notice a bird that has landed on your windowsill and without thinking recognize it as a hello sign from a loved one on the other side. Or perhaps you take a wrong turn down a dead end street and instead of becoming frustrated you realize that this is a sign that a recent idea you have been contemplating at work may not be viable.

When encounters such as these begin to happen you slowly become aware that you are no longer living in a meaningless and impersonal world. You wake to the presence of an unceasing divine and holy communion where you are loved, guided, and tended to, and you realize that you are held within the embrace of a mysterious and all-encompassing web of life.

A greater presence and power is calling to you and reaching out to offer you support, comfort, laughter, direction, and enlightenment. How can you refuse?

PART 3

LIVING ORACLE GLOSSARY OF SIGNS

Throughout time, there have been philosophers and enlightened teachers who have suggested that the world around us is not as real as we may believe it to be. It has been suggested that all we experience in the physical world is just a fleeting dream. Through this lens, everything we encounter can become a silent messenger that awakens us to a new perception, understanding of ourselves and life, and empowers us to perceive another world, another reality, much more eternal than this.

This glossary will assist you in interpreting the signs and symbols that you receive in the Living Oracle exercises. It contains many of the mundane and everyday objects, things, people, and activities that you may encounter as you cast the Sign Oracles. Allow it to guide and wake you.

CHAPTER 11

TYPES OF TRANSPORTATION

You will likely encounter many different types of vehicles and modes of transportation while casting the Living Oracle. Not every vehicle that you encounter is a sign or message. Listen to your intuition and look for confirming signs and patterns. For example, vehicles with license plates that contain letters that are significant to you or a line of vehicles of the same color may be signs. If a vehicle feels like a sign to you, accept it as one.

Types of transportation are symbolic of our psyche, our ego, our physical self, and our spirit. They indicate how we move through life, our journey, and our path forward. They also offer guidance and insight into our choices and possibilities and what is to come.

AIRPLANE

An airplane can indicate rising above current problems and issues, the need or ability to see the big picture, expansion of consciousness, taking flight, or leaving your current situation. It can also be a confirming message that you are communicating and connecting to your guides, helpers, and loved ones in the spirit realm.

Air Force Jet

An air force jet is a sign of organization, a united approach, precision, and purpose. It is a message to pay attention to your current situation and approach any issues or problems with a clear plan of action. Use your intelligence and think things through with someone you trust. It can indicate the need to rise above the current problem and situation and perceive it through a higher perspective.

Small, Private Plane

A small plane is a sign of self-empowerment and using your higher thought and insights to guide you. A small plane indicates that you can rely on and trust your wisdom and higher self.

Ambulance

An ambulance is a message that you need to take care of yourself and heal any physical, mental, emotional, or spiritual wounds. If the lights of the ambulance are flashing and it speeds by you, it is a sign of the urgency of your situation. It may also indicate healing gifts and that your life purpose may involve healing and helping others.

Armored Car

An armored car represents locked-away abundance and inner riches. This is a sign to share, open your heart, and let go of defensiveness. If you are starting a new business, career, or project, it may indicate the need to be financially conservative and be a warning against overspending.

Bicycle

A bicycle is a sign of balance, freedom, and personal effort. It is a message that you are in charge of where you are going and your progress in getting there. It may also be a message to be flexible and avoid extremes in work and pleasure. If you have been pushing yourself, it may be time to take a more leisurely approach.

Broken Bicycle

A broken or old bike can be a sign to delay plans, pause, and think things over before taking action. It may also be a message to seek out the support of others and not to try to go it alone.

Chained or Locked on a Fixture

A bicycle that is chained or locked onto a fixture, like a telephone pole, is a sign of a lack of personal will. If you are feeling out of balance in your life, or that you have to do things a certain way, this is a message to take back your power and be true to yourself and what works for you.

Competitive

A group of competitive riders can be a message to pay attention to the people around you—acquaintances, friends, or coworkers. Be alert in your relationships and be careful not to be overly assertive, combative, or pushy. It may also indicate that you are in a competitive environment and need to be in top form.

BOAT

A boat is a sign of emotional balance, spirituality, and the ability to let go and trust unseen forces. The condition of the water must be considered an important aspect to the sign.

A boat in choppy water may be a message to keep steady during times of emotional upheaval and ups and downs. In placid, still waters, a boat is a message of peace and tranquility. If the water is dark or muddy, it is a message of emotional negativity and confusion. Clear water indicates heart-centered awareness and spiritual attainment.

Canoe

A canoe or kayak is a sign of your personal spiritual and emotional journey. It is a message to listen to your heart and soul and seek what is right for you. It may indicate the need to go with the flow and to beware of any emotional upheavals or stresses and handle them with precision and care.

Car Pulling Boat

A car pulling a boat is a sign that you may need to devote time to getting in touch with your emotions and feelings and to be honest with yourself about what you want. There may be repressed emotions that are weighing you down and preventing you from perceiving and enjoying what is being offered.

Fishing Boat

A fishing boat is a message that you may need emotional and spiritual care. Take the time to understand your needs and know that there is an abundance of love and support from the spirit realm available to you. Be sincere in your efforts and patient with the results.

Sailboat

A sailboat is a message to take the path of least resistance. Find what works for you and go with it. Even if others do not understand, trust your sense of what is right for you. A sailboat may also be a sign to trust your intuitive and psychic insight and impressions. Your individuality and freedom is important right now.

BUS

While a car or bicycle is symbolic of going forward in an individual way, a bus represents collective consciousness or your connection with others. Buses may be a sign of your role in the family, workplace, community, or world. They indicate the collective whole rather than personal or intimate relationships.

Pay attention to any signs or billboards on a bus. It may be that the message is in what the bus is advertising.

City Bus

A city bus may be a message to focus on friendships, work relationships, and your connection with your neighbors or the community. If you have been feeling as if you do not matter or that you are not seen or known, a city bus reminds you that your presence and contribution are essential. As you contribute to others' needs or welfare, you make progress on your life plan.

Church Bus

A church bus is a message to connect spiritually with others or to express your spirituality or be of service to others in your community. It may also be a message to practice what you preach.

School Bus

A school bus is a sign that you are learning important life lessons through your connection and relationships with others. If you are confused or unsure of how to deal a current problem or if you have a pressing decision, focus on the lesson that you are learning through it. The situation will then resolve itself. A school bus may also be a message to go back to school or a sign to teach others.

CAMPER

A camper is a sign of self-sufficiency and the need for independence. It is a message to let go of the past and move forward. You have all that you need to create and manifest what you desire. It may also indicate the need to take time in the outdoors and nature or to go inward and explore your individuality.

CAR

A car is symbolic of your individual path through life, your drive, ambition, and transitioning from one stage of life to another. A car may also represent your physical self.

Dents, Scratches

A car with dents and scratches or in need of bodywork may be a sign of difficulties and the stress and strain that it has had on you. A dented beatup-looking car may indicate the need to physically or emotionally heal and take better care of yourself. A car may also be a sign of a wounded ego and feeling picked on, or a message to pay attention to how you are treating others.

Compact Car

A compact car may indicate the need to downsize your expectations or goals. Be modest and content with what is and with what is being offered. Power is in the small. This is not the time to take risks; go with the practical.

Convertible

A convertible may be a message to free yourself from negative beliefs, judgments, and thoughts. Open your mind to higher thoughts and allow the light of spiritual wisdom to expand your consciousness. It is also a sign of freedom and enjoyment and allowing yourself to let go.

Junk Car

A car that has been junked or is no longer operational can indicate that a present issue or concern is not viable. If you have a question about a relationship, new career path, or new undertaking, this is a warning of heartache or a disappointing outcome.

Limousine

A limousine symbolizes self-worth, the ego, materialism, and superficialities. Limit your expectations of others and share the good that comes your way. This is not the time to allow pride or grandiose ideas to cloud your judgment. Be humble and accepting.

Alternatively, it may be a sign of coming success, financial wealth, or the need to celebrate a special occasion.

Luxury Car

A luxury car like a Rolls-Royce is a sign of ambition and self-worth. It is a message to be careful not to judge yourself or others by external status symbols and superficial materialism. If you have been feeling stressed about finances, this may be a message of improvement and coming abundance.

Minivan

A minivan can be a sign to focus on family, coworkers, and friends and to consider their place in your life. They may be helpful in supporting you in attaining your goals. A minivan may also be a message to go along with the group and give up your personal aims and desires to support others.

New Car

A new car may be a sign of a new path, beginning, or direction. Renewal in some form is making its way into your life. The color of the car may offer more insight.

Speeding Car

A speeding car can be a symbol to get going and move forward. If the car is recklessly speeding, it is a warning of danger or a message to slow down. It can also indicate that you do not have control or that you are moving too quickly in some area of your life.

Sports Car

A sports car may be a sign that you are neglecting or sacrificing pleasure and a sense of adventure for the status quo and routine. You may need to take a little more risk and get out of your comfort zone. Alternatively, this may be a message to focus on the practical matters of everyday life.

Vintage Car

A vintage car that has been restored and is in good condition may represent healing from past issues and difficulties and overcoming illness. It is a positive message of renewal and improvement.

Encountering a vintage car that is in the process of being restored or is non-functional is a message to become aware of family and past family generational behaviors, beliefs, patterns, and habits that may be adversely affecting you in the present. Let go of and heal dysfunctional old family patterns that are holding you back.

DELIVERY TRUCKS

A delivery truck may indicate present or coming change and the arrival of a material or a spiritual gift. It may also be a sign of a relationship, project, or desire in the beginning stages of manifestation. Something is coming your way.

Alcohol

A beer or alcohol delivery truck is a sign that you may not be seeing something clearly. You may be in a dreamlike or delusional state or in denial about someone or what is happening in your life. It may be a message to confront and face your current situation for what it is rather than what you would like it to be. This may also be a pun reminding you of the presence of "spirits" close by.

Building Materials

A truck delivering building supplies may be a sign of rejuvenation and renewal of mind, body, and spirit. It is time to rebuild your life. You will be helped and supported by the spiritual realm and friends, family, and others in the physical world. It may also be a sign to take care of your physical health, improve your diet, and begin an exercise routine.

Florist

Flower delivery is sign of a spiritual gift of love or romance and new love coming your way.

Food

A food delivery truck represents nourishment or something that feeds the soul and spirit coming into your life. A truck with fresh vegetables and fruit can be more literal and indicate the need to improve your diet.

Furniture

A furniture or appliance delivery truck may indicate the need to adopt new attitudes and beliefs and to let go of outdated habits and limiting thoughts. It may also be a more literal message of changes in your home or home life.

Mail Truck

A mail, UPS, FedEx, or other mail or package delivery truck may be a sign that much-needed insights, information, or communication is coming your way. You may also have information or insights that others need. This may come through an intuitive or psychic gift. It might also point to your ability to intuit messages for yourself and others and communicate with the other side.

FIRE ENGINE

A fire engine can indicate a past, present, or future troubling or intense issue or situation that may be causing worry and stress. Although you may be at a loss as what to do, there will be a positive outcome. You are being guided and helped by spiritual forces.

Speeding by with Lights Flashing

If a fire engine is speeding past you with its lights flashing, it is a sign of the urgency of your situation. You may need expert help from others to solve a problem.

GOLF CART

A golf cart may be a sign that you have a lackadaisical and leisurely approach to issues and your personal growth. If you feel that you may be procrastinating, this is a sign to get moving. Alternatively, if you have been working long hours or involved in a stressful situation this can be a message that you need to take some time for leisure and relaxation.

HEARSE

A hearse may be a message that a relationship, job, condition, or project is completed or coming to an end. It may also be a warning to not go forward with a relationship or venture. A loved one on the other side might also use a hearse to get your attention to let you know that he or she is with you and would like to further communicate with you.

HEAVY EQUIPMENT,
PLOW, BACKHOE, BOBCAT

Heavy equipment may be a sign of your power and ability to transform and change your current situation. If you have been sitting on the sidelines and waiting for something to happen, this is a message to take action and get involved. You have what it takes to create something positive. If you are actively pursuing change, success is coming.

HELICOPTER

A helicopter is a sign that spiritual help and assistance are close by. There are no situations, conditions, or areas that the spirit realm cannot access or influence. All you need to do is ask.

A helicopter can also be a message to not overestimate the time and energy that a new project or a current situation may take. If you are wavering over how much to give to something or someone, pull back and reassess what you will get in return.

MOTORCYCLE

A motorcycle is a sign of individuality and a message to be bold, take a risk, and move forward on a project, idea, or relationship. Trust yourself and go it alone if you need to.

MOVING VAN

A moving van is a sign that it is time to make a drastic change. This may have to do with your goals, desires, career, health, or a relationship. This may also be a sign to change your perspective or view of reality, and let go of the beliefs and thoughts that may be limiting and hindering your progress. If you are thinking of moving or selling your home, this is a positive sign.

POLICE CAR

A police car is a sign that you have been giving your power away to an outer authority. It may also be a message that you need to become more aware of your leadership and expertise in an area that is of interest to you. This may also be a sign to pay attention to rules, regulations, and outer guidelines.

Recreational Vehicle

A recreational vehicle can represent fun, adventure, and may be a message to express personality traits, talents, and aspects of your individuality that you may normally keep hidden. It may also be a message to further explore your options before making a decision.

Scooter

A scooter is a sign of balancing vulnerability and strength. You are strong enough to be yourself and express your truth. At the same time be aware that you may not receive the support and understanding from others that is due you. Although you may feel misunderstood, this is temporary. Keep moving forward.

Subway

A subway is a message that unconscious desires, beliefs, or thoughts may be motivating and driving your behavior. If you experiencing conditions and situations that are not satisfying or are confusing, look within. There is a lot going on behind the scenes that you may not be aware of. A subway may also be a message to express and acknowledge your gifts and talents.

Taxi

A taxi is a sign that you may need to ask foor enlist help or guidance from another. A trusted friend, therapist, or career mentor may be able to assist you in reaching your goal or guide you. Let others in and trust their direction.

Tractor

A tractor is symbolic of strength, purpose, and powerful advance. With determination and work you can succeed in whatever undertaking or area you may be interested in. Alternatively, it may also indicate heavy burdens and responsibility. While it is important to support others, be sure that you are not taking on worries and stress of others.

Farm Tractor

A farm tractor or a tractor carrying farm animals can be a message that you possess the ability to provide and care for others in a powerful way. It may also be a warning to watch your diet and eat healthy foods.

Tractor-Trailer

A tractor-trailer symbolizes the ability to be successful in a large-scale project or undertaking. If the tractor-trailer is carrying cars, it may be a message that your purpose may be to help others to move forward or to be a guide to others.

A tractor-trailer on the side of the road indicates a need to pause on a large-scale project or goal before going forward.

An empty tractor-trailer is a sign of confusion and not knowing your purpose and life path. It indicates that you are not fully using and engaged in your talents and abilities. You have a lot to give and the inner reserves to make it.

TRAIN

Trains represent steady progress, a focused mind and self-will, and pre-destination. They may also be a message that there is a higher power directing your path.

A speeding train is a message to proceed and trust your plans. It is a positive sign of progress.

Stopping for a train is a message that frustrations or obstacles are only temporary. Be patient as the way is being opened up for you.

Train Tracks

Train tracks suggest making conservative choices, following an accepted method, and not taking risks.

Train tracks that are obsolete and no longer used may indicate that you have a one-track mind and need to consider other options.

Train Station

Encountering a train station is a message to consider your plans, organize yourself, and get input from others. It may also indicate becoming busy and overwhelmed with options and choices. It is a suggestion to stay focused and be careful that you do not get distracted.

Train Whistle

Hearing a train whistle is a warning to review your choices and decisions and make sure that they support your highest good.

TRUCK

Trucks represent service to others, strength, responsibilities, the ability to work hard, or that there is work to be done. Trucks can be an omen of coming abundance and they may symbolize your career path.

Cable Truck

A cable or Internet service truck or a truck laying or repairing cable lines indicates communication, increased social interactions, and reaching out to others. This may also be a sign from the spirit realm encouraging you to develop your medium abilities.

Electrical Repair Truck

An electrician's repair truck or a crew working on electrical lines may indicate that you have latent healing abilities, especially energy or hands-on healing. It may be a sign encouraging you to be of service to others in this way or a sign that you or someone you love may be in need of healing.

Loved ones on the other side often work through electrical energy to let us know that they are present. Electrical lines may also be a sign from a loved one, letting you know that he or she is present.

Dump Truck

A dump truck represents letting go, detoxing, and highlights the need to transform through releasing what is no longer in your highest good.

Garbage Truck

A garbage truck is a message that you may be taking on others' negativity, problems, and worries. You may not be aware of it, but the energy of others may be affecting your mood, health, stress levels, and sense of well-being. To make it easier to fully benefit from the inherent goodness within all of life, trust in a meaningful universe that knows and cares for you.

Pickup Truck

A pickup truck is a message to get to work on those things that are most meaningful and important to you. If you have been supporting others' dreams and goals, it is time to focus on you.

Recycling Truck

A recycling truck is a message to accept all of who you are. If you are feeling guilt or a lack of self-worth for past actions or experiences, forgive yourself. Learn from the lessons that life has sent your way and use this wisdom and awareness to create more of what you desire.

Tow Truck

A tow truck that is not pulling a car may be a sign of your ability to be of assistance to another and that you have more strength than what you are aware of.

A tow truck towing a car can be a sign that another's burdens and responsibilities are weighing on you. It is a sign to let go of others' negativity and opinions.

Utilities Truck

A utilities truck represents focusing on the basics, being pragmatic, and a message to get to work in practical ways on your dreams and aspirations.

CHAPTER 12

ROADS

Roads are a common and important bearer of signs and messages in the Living Oracle. They symbolize your current path, your past, and where you are going. They also foretell the ease, obstacles, and twists and turns that you may encounter in the future.

While casting an oracle, you will likely encounter many roads. Those that embody signs and messages will draw your attention and may have other confirming signs associated with them. Trust your intuition and gut feelings.

CROSSROAD

A crossroad indicates that you need to make a conscious change. You cannot stay on the path that you have been on. New opportunities and possibilities are present; be willing to accept them.

CROSSWALK

A crosswalk is a sign that there are outer influences that you need to be aware of. Be careful in your dealings with others. People may not act in predictable ways or do or say what you expect them to.

CUL-DE-SAC

A cul-de-sac or fork in the road is a message that your current path may not be rewarding or provide you with the opportunities or outcome that you hope for. It may also be a message to find and stay in your comfort zone for the time being.

GRAVEL

A gravel road is a sign of minor irritations and slow going in the present and near future. It is a message to take your time and not become discouraged. It may also be a message to try something new.

HIGHWAY

A highway is a sign that you will soon be making progress and building momentum. It is a message to follow convention and go with the flow.

A highway underpass indicates overthinking and chaotic thoughts. It is a message to listen to your heart, not your head.

A highway exit ramp is a message to veer away from the accepted norm and take a more creative approach. If you have been indecisive it is time to make a choice or decision and commit. An exit ramp may also be a sign that you are about to reach a goal.

POTHOLES

Potholes are a sign to be aware of detail and what appear to be minor irritations. Although the issues you are confronting are not necessarily significant, they still have the ability to cause stress and setbacks. Don't just let things go, follow up on issues as they arise.

ROAD CONSTRUCTION

Encountering construction workers, working on roads or in other public places, is a sign that you may need help, guidance, and support from others to move forward in creating and fulfilling your dreams and desires. This may also be a sign to be there for others and help them to build their dreams.

ROADBLOCK

A roadblock can be a warning sign. The spirit realm may be trying to give you the message to reconsider your plans. Stop and assess your situation, relationship, career plans, or whatever your concern may be. You may need more information before going forward.

SPEED BUMP

A speed bump is a sign of an unexpected obstacle or hurdle. It is a message to slow down and be attentive to what is in front of you. As you take care of details and minor problems, you gain clarity and go forward with ease.

TRAFFIC CIRCLE

A traffic circle or roundabout is a sign of options and easy transition onto a new path. If you feel that you are going in circles, it is temporary. Be alert to possibilities and choose the path of least resistance.

WALKING PATH

A walking path is a sign to make progress toward your desires and goals you need solitude and to listen within. A path in the woods or through trees and vegetation is a sign of entering into the unknown— the inner mystery of self. This journey can only be undertaken solo. You may need to go it alone, at least for a while.

WINDING ROAD

A winding road is a message of slow progress and twists and turns along the way. Whatever your concern may be, the outcome will not be straightforward.

CHAPTER 13

ROAD SIGNS AND BUSINESS SIGNS

You will likely encounter many different signs when practicing the Living Oracle. Not all the signs that you come across will be messages from the spirit realm. Use intuitive symbolic awareness and your gut intuition to determine what signs are significant for you.

ROAD SIGNS

Many street signs are straightforward and mean what they say. Look to other signs and messages in close proximity to the signs that may add additional information to the street sign.

Caution

A yellow caution sign may be a direct message to be cautious, aware, and attentive. Even if you feel confident and self-assured, you may want to review your current circumstances and choices before moving forward.

Construction Area

A construction area sign can be a message to get to work and focus on an idea, problem, goal, or issue. It may be time to take action on something that you have been thinking, planning, or wondering about.

Dead-End

Encountering a dead-end sign or walking down a dead-end road is a direct message that whatever your area of concern may be, it is not viable or a good idea to pursue it. It's time for new direction.

Detour

A detour sign may be a message from the spirit realm letting you know that your current plans or desires may not proceed as planned. It can also be a message that you may not be experiencing what you desire because something better is coming your way. If you encounter a detour sign, let go of your expectations, listen within, and follow where you feel led, even if it does not make sense.

Flashing Lights

When you see flashing streetlights you are being alerted to a situation or condition that you may not recognize as important or significant. Flashing yellow lights are a sign of caution, while flashing red lights are a sign to stop and assess what is driving and motivating your choices and behavior before going forward.

Intersection Ahead

If you encounter an intersection ahead sign, it may be a message of present or future conflict or opposition. This may be with another person, an institution, or an inner conflict. Let go of your ego and need to be right. Consider all sides and you will come to a resolution. An intersection ahead sign might also refer to a recent choice you made that you may need to rethink.

No Parking

A no parking sign is message that you have not yet discovered what you are looking for or what you need. Don't talk yourself into something that you know in your gut is not right for you. Keep moving forward and don't get complacent.

Pedestrian Crossing

A pedestrian crossing sign is a message that despite appearances a way is being made for you. If you are confronting difficulties or in a situation that looks like the odds are against you, you will soon experience ease and clarity. This may also be a message that someone will soon be entering your life who will have a positive impact on you.

Railroad Crossing

A railroad crossing sign is a message to use reasoning and logic and weigh practicalities with your hopes and wishes. A current issue or condition needs decisive thinking and a direct approach.

School Zone

When you encounter a school zone sign, the spirit realm is sending you the message to become aware of the lesson behind present conditions and to learn from your mistakes and current situation. You may not realize it, but you can attain a higher level of wisdom and insight through what you are experiencing.

Slow

Another direct message, a slow sign is a message to literally slow down. You may need to take better care of yourself physically, mentally, emotionally, or spiritually. Even if you are making progress and everything seems to be going the way you would like it to, this is a message to be aware and alert to coming change or an issue that needs your attention.

Soft Shoulder

A soft shoulder sign is a message from the spirit realm letting you know that they are with you. Although you may feel as if you are going through challenges alone, you are not. You are seen, loved, and cared for. A spiritual "soft shoulder" to lean on is present.

Stop

A stop sign is a clear and direct message to stop and reassess a goal, ideal, relationship, expectation, or desire. If you are contemplating a change or new venture, this is not the time to go forward. If you are reminiscing about the past or contemplating the future, stay in present time.

A four-way stop sign is a more powerful alert to reconsider your current choices and the path that you are on.

Winding Road

Encountering a winding road sign is a message of twists and turns in conditions—past, present, and future. Although it may feel as if you are having to deal with delays, obstructions, or hindrances, you are making positive progress. This may also be a suggestion to relax and unwind.

BUSINESS SIGNS

Signs on businesses should be interpreted in connection with other confirming signs. For instance, business signs may be a message if the number of the building or numbers on the sign have a personal meaning or synchronicity. The type of business is also important. For instance, a restaurant sign will have a different meaning than a clothing store sign. (See *Buildings* and *Numbers*.)

Buy One, Get One Free

A buy one, get one free sign is a sign of increase and abundance. Your efforts are being supported and now is a good time to commit or take action. What you give will come back to you tenfold. Although a positive sign, keep in mind that negative thoughts or actions will also return back to you in abundance.

Closed

A closed sign can be a message that something is not available to you at this time. This may be an opportunity or desired outcome. It might also be an aspect of yourself that you have denied or pushed away; for instance, a closed heart or a lack of forgiveness. The building that the sign is on will give you clues as to the area the message is intended for.

For Rent or Lease

A for rent or lease sign is a message that your situation is temporary. It might also be a suggestion to try something new, be flexible, and adapt to others' needs and desires while remaining true to your authentic self.

For Sale

A for sale sign is a message that something is being offered to you or that you have something to offer others. This may be a unique gift that you possess or a skill or ability. It might also be your compassion, love, or healing energy that you are being asked to contribute. A for sale sign may also be a message to value yourself, your time, and your energy, and be mindful to maintain the balance of give and take with others.

Free

A reminder that the best things in life will come to you naturally and with ease. A free sign is encouraging you to accept the love, abundance, and joy that is freely being offered you.

Going Out of Business

A going out of business sign is letting you know that it is time to let go of what no longer serves your highest good. If you have been frustrated or working hard without a sense of fulfillment or progress, this is a message to move on. Cut your losses and know that something better is on its way.

Grand Opening

A grand opening sign is a message of transformation and emergence. A new you is unfolding and ready to be expressed. It is time for the authentic you to step out into the world and share your unique and special gifts.

Limited Time Only

When you encounter a limited time only sign, this is a message to seize a present opportunity or one that will be coming your way. If you are going through challenges or difficulties, this can be a message that it will not last for long. Conditions will soon improve.

Liquidation Sale

A liquidation sale sign is a message to focus on your emotions and feel any feelings that you may have suppressed or ignored. It is a reminder that there is value in taking time to heal old wounds and past pain. As you feel your feelings, they dissipate and make room for new, revitalizing emotions and feelings.

Open

An open sign is a message to open your mind, heart, and spirit, and allow new ideas, thoughts, conditions, and people into your life. Enjoy the freedom that comes when you allow yourself to experience life as it is, one day and one moment at a time.

Welcome

When you encounter a welcome sign, the spirit realm is inviting you into a deeper connection and communion. This is an affirmation that you are loved and seen and watched over. An angel, loved one, spirit guide, or other spirit being is present and guiding you.

CHAPTER 14

BUILDINGS

Depending on the sign casting location, you may encounter a few or many buildings. Not all of the buildings that you observe are significant. Intuitive and symbolic awareness will help you to discern if a building is a sign or message. It is also helpful to look for a confirming synchronicity. For instance, does the number of the building have a personal or symbolic meaning to you? Is there a feather, coins, or other personal symbolic signs close to or near the building? Do you observe any patterns or repeating signs connected to or close to the building? Does your intuition tell you that the building is a sign?

In general, buildings represent our perception of ourselves in the world, how others perceive us, finances, work, and practical and material concerns.

ACCOUNTANT OFFICE

Encountering an accountant's office, may be a message to pay attention to details, especially with finances. It might also be a reminder that you are responsible for what you say and do. All things come to us in the karmic equal measure of what we put into motion.

APARTMENT

An apartment complex may be a message to consider how much others influence your decisions and sense of self. If you are overwhelmed with responsibilities and feeling pressure to please others, this a sign to focus on your individuality and true self.

This may also be a sign to create balance with others. If you are a loner or currently at odds with someone, this can be a message to focus on what you have in common and what connects you to others.

A highrise apartment building is a sign to become aware of the influence that others have over you. If you feel that your inner light is being blocked, let it shine.

ART GALLERY

An art gallery is a message to focus on your creativity, free your mind and heart, and open to greater possibilities. Success will come as you create a vision of your life that is based on your authentic self.

Art being sold on the street or in a park is a message to express and share your unique and creative self with others and the world. It is also a message to let go of your criticism and judgments of self and others. Celebrate and enjoy your individuality and allow others to freely express their truth in the ways they choose.

ATTORNEY OFFICE

An attorney office may be a message to pay attention to loose ends, processes, and details, especially in legal, property, and business issues. It may also indicate the need to seek the advice of another for direction and to help you to decipher a confusing situation. If you are currently involved in a legal situation, look for confirming signs to better foretell the outcome.

BANK

A bank is a sign to focus on finances, abundance, resources, or self-worth. The message may be to become more conscious and aware of spending, saving, and sharing, or receiving money or other resources. It may also point to less tangible material finances and instead be a sign to become aware of and improve or heal your personal sense of worth and value.

BAR

A bar is a sign to make sure that your connections and relationships with others are based on integrity and authenticity. You may need to get away from the pressures and stresses of daily life. Just be alert to falsities and deceit in social situations.

BOOKSTORE

A bookstore is a message to explore new ideas, be creative, and welcome new possibilities into your life. You may need inspiration to get out of a rut or routine. A bookstore may also be a sign to write and may be announcing literary success.

CHURCH

Encountering a church is a sign of spirituality, divine presence, and sharing your spirituality with others. It can also be a message of group spiritual activity or the beliefs and dogma that are imposed on ourselves and others.

People going in or out of a church is a message that now or in the near future you will experience an increase in spiritual activity with others or with a group.

CLOTHING STORE

A clothing store is a sign of changing attitudes, ideas, and opinions. It is a message to be flexible, open to change, and to allow others to be who they are. It may be time to try new things and express new aspects of your authentic self.

CONVENIENCE STORE

A convenience store is a sign of a quick and easy solution to a current concern or problem. What you need will be provided and it may come to you through another. It can also be a message to be careful to not simply skim over issues and difficulties. Look deeper into yourself and what is happening in your life.

COURTHOUSE

A courthouse is a message to be up front and honest in your dealings with others. If you feel as if you have been dealt with unfairly or misjudged, this is also a sign that justice will come to you in some form.

DAYCARE

A daycare is a message of innocence and the happiness that comes from the small things in life. Allow your inner child out and experience more playfulness and whimsy. A daycare can also be a message to let go of an immature and self-centered perspective.

DENTIST OFFICE

A dentist office is a message to improve communication and be careful with what you say to others. If you are in a relationship, it may indicate verbal abuse and painful criticism. A dentist office may also be a direct sign to see a dentist or take better care of your teeth.

DEPARTMENT STORE

A department store is a sign to carefully review your available choices and options before making a decision. If you are tempted to act impulsively, be sure that your wants and desires serve your highest good.

DILAPIDATED BUILDING

When you encounter a dilapidated building, this is a sign that you or someone you know is in need of physical, emotional, or mental help and healing. There may be long-ignored issues and pain that is causing current health, and other, issues.

FIRE STATION

A fire station is a message to be aware, alert, and cautious when dealing with small problems. This is not the time to provoke or add fuel to existing issues and problems. Be a calming influence in the midst of tense and stressful situations.

FUNERAL HOME

A funeral home may be a message that your current plans are not viable. Honor your past; it is over. Even though you may not know what the future holds, a new you is emerging. Direction may be disguised as loss. May also be a message of completion and a suggestion to honor and celebrate the past and how far you have come.

FURNITURE STORE

Furniture is symbolic of your conscious self and outer personality. A furniture store is a message that your day-to-day habits, routines, and outer life may not be expressing your true self and core values. You are going through a period of change. Allow aspects of your personality that better express your true self to surface.

GAS STATION

A gas station is a sign of the habits and unconscious beliefs that may be either beneficially increasing or robbing you of energy and stamina. If you continually feel tired or drained, it may be due to repressed feelings of fear or worthlessness. To go forward with your goals and desires, you may need to let go of negativity and generate more positive life-giving energy. This may also be a sign that you may be exerting effort and energy with people or in a situation that is draining your resources.

GROCERY STORE

A grocery store is a sign to nurture others and receive nurturing and care from others. If you have been feeling restricted or in a rut, a grocery store is a message that the universe operates through abundance and possibilities. A grocery store can also be a message to pay better attention to your dietary needs and how what you eat and drink affects your health.

HEALTH CLUB/GYM

Encountering a health club or gym is a message to focus on yourself and your health and emotional, mental, or spiritual well-being. It may also be a sign to take disciplined action and steps in reaching your goals. If you have been lazy or procrastinating, this is a motivating sign to put effort into creating what you desire.

HOSPITAL

A hospital can be a sign from the spirit realm encouraging you to get a health checkup or that you are in need of mind/body/spirit healing. This is a sign that you may need professional or expert help or support.

It can also be a message that you have a gift for healing and helping others, especially in the area of health and well-being. A hospital may also indicate the need to take a bigger role in contributing to the betterment and improvement of local and global issues.

HOTEL

A hotel is a sign of a temporary situation, a transition, or a reawakening that results in a new sense of self. Whatever you are currently experiencing is soon to change. Resist holding on and go with the flow. Now is the time to think positive thoughts and perceive what is happening through a clearer lens.

JAIL/PRISON

Passing a jail or prison is a sign of being restricted, confined, stifled, or controlled. It is important to let go of any inner beliefs, feelings, or old wounds that may be limiting and controlling you. If there are any situations, people, or expectations that are keeping you from living authentically and joyfully, free yourself.

A jail or prison may also be a sign to release unconscious feelings of guilt or harsh or critical judgments of self or others that may be blocking you from receiving love and joy.

JEWELRY STORE

Encountering a jewelry store may be a sign that a gift from nature spirits and the heavens has come or is coming your way. It may also be a message to commit and devote yourself to another or to a higher service or cause.

LIQUOR STORE

A liquor store is a message to keep things in perspective and balance. If you are stressed and anxious, loosen up and relax. If you feel a little lost without direction, establish step-by-step goals. It can also indicate that you or someone close to you may have a problem with alcohol.

MUSEUM

A museum is a message to perceive the value and worth of your past, even the challenging and difficult times. Have gratitude for and become aware of how the past has benefited you. Alternatively, if you are over-idealizing and clinging to the past, let it go and be in the present.

OFFICE COMPLEX

An office building is a sign to be practical, organized, and create order in your life. This may have to do with work, finances, or your home environment. It may also be a sign that the spirit realm is aligned and supporting your efforts to bring peace to chaos and emotional stress.

PARKING GARAGE

A parking garage is a message that you may need to wait before moving forward with plans or desires. There are outer forces that are influencing what is possible right now. Be patient, rest, and take some time for yourself.

PAWN SHOP

A pawn shop symbolizes self-worth and is a message not to compromise who you are or what you value for immediate pleasure or need. It may also imply that there is an imbalance in a current issue or condition that will eventually result in loss.

POLICE STATION

A police station is a message to be honest, truthful, and come clean to yourself and others. Forgive yourself and forgive others for any intentional or unintentional slights or hurtful words or actions. This may also be a message to be cautious with authority figures. If you are an authority figure of some kind, this may be a message to be firm but benevolent.

PUBLIC RESTROOM

A public restroom is a sign to let go of cultural standards, beliefs, or expectations that may not be supportive and aligned with your true self. This may also be a message that you are able to help others to let go of and release their negative thoughts, emotions, and beliefs and to detox their body and improve their health and well-being.

RESTAURANT

Symbolic of the quality of your relationships with others, a restaurant is a message to evaluate the care and nurturing that you receive from friends, family, and loved ones, and to become more conscious of the nurturing and care that you provide to others.

Fast-food

A fast-food restaurant can be a message that your relationships are shallow and lack substance. It may also imply casual sexual relationships that have no depth and may ultimately be to your determent. Seek quality and satisfying connections with others.

SCHOOL

Encountering a school may be a message from your higher self. Our challenges and daily situations and conditions contain important soul lessons that we have come here to learn. Schools are a sign to consider the current lessons in your present experiences. Once you learn the lesson, difficult situations and problems fall away.

Elementary

An elementary school is symbolic of past childhood lessons that you may need to revisit. Issues from the past may be affecting your current situation. It can also be a message to rekindle your child-like spirit or alternatively to quiet the impulsive inner child and act with maturity.

Middle or High

A middle, junior high, or high school may symbolize that you are re-belling against what life is trying to teach you. This is a message to lis-ten within for your truth. Let go of others' expectations. Can also indicate a period of challenging growth. However, this is only tempo-rary. This too shall pass.

College

A college indicates higher-level ideas, concepts, and expanding your consciousness. This may also be a sign to further your education or learn new skills. It may also indicate that you are currently learning important lessons. You are acquiring knowledge and wisdom.

If your area of concern or question involves your career or finances, a school may also be a more literal sign directing you to learn or attend school.

SEWER PLANT

A sewer plant is a sign that you may be the recipient of others' negativ-ity and toxic attitudes and beliefs. It is a wake-up call to examine the negativity in your life. Let go of it and purify your mind, body, and spirit. A sewer plant might also be a message that you have a purpose and mission to help and heal others physically, mentally, emotionally, and spiritually.

STRIP CLUB

A strip club or nude bar is a sign of empty hopes and dreams, sensuality, and sexuality. Your desires may not be anchored in your most authentic self. Become aware of any repressed feelings or thoughts that may be getting in the way of true intimacy with yourself or with another.

THEATER

A theater may be a message encouraging you to take a break from life and observe what is happening around you. It is a sign to be objective, remove yourself from the center of attention, and take a backseat for the time being. Detach from your present situation and you will gain a new perspective.

TRUCK STOP

A truck stop is a sign that you need rest and recuperation during or after a trying time of hard work, burdens, and responsibilities.

URGENT CARE/MEDICAL OFFICES

Encountering an urgent care or medical office may be a sign to pay attention to specific issues and areas of your health and well-being. Examine your life and focus on understanding what is and what is not working. Get input and advice from someone you trust. An urgent care or medical office may also indicate that in some area of your life there is something that needs your attention. Take the time to look within and enlist the help of others if needed; don't disregard or dismiss what you may think is insignificant.

VACANT BUILDING

A vacant building is a sign of creativity, new beginnings, and a fresh start. What you focus on will have an impact on and affect others. This is a positive sign of expansion and influence. Alternatively, a vacant building can also indicate the need to change and let go of something. In this way it can be a message to accept loss and move forward.

VETERINARIAN

A veterinarian office is a symbol of unconditional love and healing. It is a sign to love all of who you are, even your primal instincts and unconscious drives. A veterinary office or hospital can be a message that you or someone close to you may need emotional healing. Forgive yourself and others and practice compassion.

Animals and birds are often nature spirit messengers who reflect our own inner or dormant qualities and gifts. Loved ones on the other side, spirit guides, angels, and archangels often use animals and birds as signs. A veterinarian office can be a sign to focus on improving your connection to the spirit realm. They are helping you to heal.

CHAPTER 15

BUILDING AND HOME CONSTRUCTION

BUILDING CONSTRUCTION

Building construction is symbolic of our progress and obstacles in our career, creativity, and in our purpose and aspirations. They can also represent how others perceive us, our public image, and what we may need to know to achieve our goals and experience success.

As with the other things you may encounter in the Living Oracle, not every building that you encounter is a sign; pay attention to your intuitive feelings and confirming signs.

Construction Crew

A building construction crew represents the need to work with others to achieve your goals. This is not the time to go it alone and be the lone wolf. Instead, it is a sign to join with others of like mind and to seek out those whose skills and abilities complement your own. It may indicate that help is on the way and to accept it when it arrives.

Demolition

A building that is being demolished is a sign of impending change on a large scale. The past is over and it is time to move on to new ideas, aspirations, and dreams. If you accept that it is time to change, you can go with the flow into the new. If you resist it, you could find things falling apart around you.

Large Machinery

Encountering large construction machinery is a sign that you are about to receive help and support on a large scale. This is likely in the area of a career and life purpose, and it may indicate your ability to influence and support others. Positive energy may be coming your way from the celestial realm; pay attention to new ideas and people who come into your life.

New Signage Installed

New signs are a message that it is time to change your perception of yourself in the world or to examine what are you broadcasting out to others and the universe. Examine your thoughts and attitudes, eliminate the negative and replace it with positivity.

Revolving Door

An out-of-order or newly installed revolving door in the entrance of a building is a sign that projects, career goals, and activity with others may be slowing down. It may also be a sign that you aregoing in circles and may need to get out of the loop of old patterns and behaviors. It may be time to reflect on recent progress and rejuvenate. Seek quality and not quantity.

Steel Beams

Exposed steel beams in a building is a sign to look deeper into yourself as it relates to your goals, life purpose, and career issues. It is a message to get to the truth and go back to basics. It may be time to rebuild and seek a fresh start.

Storefront Windows

Storefront windows that are under construction or being worked on is a sign to examine personality traits, habits, or practices that may need to be improved and changed. This is a message to become more aware of what you are presenting to others and how others perceive you. It can also indicate feeling exposed or not being ready to go public with an idea or project. Don't rush, be patient, and continue to work or improving yourself and clarifying your goals.

Skyscrapers

A skyscraper being built is a sign to think big and follow your dreams. The spirit realm is watching over you and assisting you in fulfilling your purpose. It can point to a life purpose of helping others to achieve their dreams and highest aspirations.

Windows Being Cleaned

Seeing windows being cleaned on a building indicates a need to achieve clarity on your self-image, especially as it relates to your career, life purpose, or activity with others. You may not perceive your true gifts and abilities. Take some time to focus on what you truly want and be true to yourself. It may also indicate that you are not seeing another or a situation objectively. Your perception is clouded.

HOUSE CONSTRUCTION

Houses are highly symbolic. They represent our physical self and different aspects of our personalities and overall sense of self.

Fence

Seeing a fence being built is a sign that you may need to break free, try new things, or take a risk. You may be walling yourself off from others and opportunities. Alternatively, it may also be a message to create better boundaries. If you feel that others infringe on your privacy or take advantage of your generosity, you may need to allow yourself more personal space.

Foundation

Seeing work being done on the foundation of a house or someone building a foundation is a sign of the need to ground yourself and pay attention to the practical aspects of day-to-day life.

Finances, career, relationships, and your health, especially your lower back and lower organs, may need your attention.

Front Door

Work being done on a front door is a message to focus on whether or not you allow others to know the true you. If you are closed down or overly protective, it is time to let others in. Alternatively, it can be a sign to become aware of your tendency to allow others' negativity and criticism to affect you. You may need to eliminate from your life those who bring you down and rob you of your joy.

New House

Workers building a house is a sign of potential and possibilities and the start of a new life or a new orientation to life. It may also be a message to take care of your health and follow through with medical treatments or a plan for rejuvenation and healing.

Painting

Seeing a house being painted is a sign of changing moods, emotions, and attitudes for the better. It can also signify improvement in a condition or situation.

Roof

Seeing work being done on a roof is a sign of your need to review your spiritual beliefs and ideals. You may need to open your mind and accept new realities and new ways of thinking that you may not be comfortable with. It may also indicate a period of consciousness evolution and divine healing.

Windows

Encountering windows being replaced, repaired, or cleaned on a house is a sign that it is time to alter your perception of reality and question your world views and your judgments and thoughts about others. How you see the world and others may be limiting your emotional, mental, spiritual, and physical well-being. It's time to see the beauty and happiness that life is offering you.

Chapter 16

Animals, Birds, Fish, and Insects

Since the beginning of recorded time, animals, birds, fish, and insects have been providing us with messages, insight, and guidance. Different cultures have endowed specific symbolic and energetic significance to all living creatures. Animals share the physical world with us, and impact and express our soulful journey as well.

Because the Living Oracle is primarily cast in urban areas, it is important to pay attention to any animals, birds, fish, or insects that you encounter. Along with living animals, drawings, signs, and symbols that illustrate animals are also signs.

Ants

Ants are a message that hard work will yield positive results. If you feel that your efforts are not seen or are disregarded, ants are a sign that this is temporary. Abundance and positive results are coming your way. Ants might also be a sign that you are capable of more than what you may think.

Alligator/Crocodile

An alligator symbolizes raw primal strength, conservatism, and protection. If you encounter an alligator as a sign, it is a message to keep things simple and trust your instincts. You may be feeling sensitive or in a situation or condition where it is important to be sensitive to others' needs. Be careful not to lash out, and give others the benefit of the doubt. Stick to what works as this is not a time to change or go forward with a new venture or project.

ARMADILLO

An armadillo is a sign of sensitivity and the need to protect your inner self. There may be people in your life or a situation that my be detrimental or harmful to your well-being. Practice detachment and objectivity.

BEAR

A bear is a sign of strength, independence, and the need for solitude and introspection. A positive sign of renewal after challenges, the bear awakens you to your inner power and capabilities. It is time to take risks and step into the unknown.

BEE, HORNET, OR WASP

Bees, hornets, or wasps are a sign of working toward a goal, being organized, and communicating clearly. If you feel as if your goals and dreams are taking a long time to manifest, they bring you the message to jump in and make it happen. Be determined and focused. Communicate your needs and plans, especially with family and in your workplace.

A bee, hornet, or wasp may also be a sign to not take an unkind remark or action from another personally. Let it go and move on.

BEAVER

A beaver is a sign of productivity, teamwork, and planning. It is a message that success will come as you put your creativity and ingenuity into action. The beaver also highlights your strengths and abilities and is a sign that you are capable of more than what you may think you are.

BIRDS

During the Living Oracle exercise you will likely see many birds. Birds that are a sign or have a message for you will come close, follow you, sweep down in front of you, and work to get your attention.

Bluebird

A sign of love, happiness, and joy, bluebirds bring you the message that grace is presently at work in your life.

Bluejay

Bluejays bring you clarity to better understand your present situation. They may be a sign to take action on your higher truth. Because blue-jays are territorial, they may be a sign to take care of yourself and be cautious.

Cardinal

The cardinal brings you the message to assess your positive accomplishments and achievements and celebrate your successes. Increase your confidence and trust yourself. If you are in the midst of a challenging situation, the cardinal brings you strength and courage.

Crow

The crow comes to tell you to be both adaptable and to move directly toward your goals. Think creatively, use your intelligence and whatever tools, skills, and abilities you have at your disposal. The crow is also a trickster that brings you the message of something unexpected coming your way.

Dove

The dove is a sign of higher consciousness and peace. It brings the gift of spiritual awareness and insight. Take a deep breath, release stress and tension, and know that you are bing led.

Duck

Ducks are a sign to lie low and take a more supportive role for the time being. There may be a current or coming situation or change that may be unsettling or irritating. This is a temporary issue that will pass. If you see a duck in the water, this is a positive message of manifestation and prosperity.

Eagle

The eagle is a sign of spiritual power and nobility. The eagle offers you protection and insight to make good, sound judgments. You are in a time of great power; encountering an eagle is a sign to rise to the occasion and express your highest vision of self. Seeing an eagle in flight is a sign that a powerful opportunity is coming your way.

Goose

Geese ask you to be sure that the path that you are on is your own. We often compromise and allow others to sway our opinions and influence our actions. Look into your heart and feel what is true for you. A flock of geese symbolize lifelong companionship and are a message that you are never alone; your spiritual loved ones are close.

Goldfinch

The goldfinch is a sign of positivity and joy. If you have been allowing negativity, boredom, or routine to dampen your spirits, a goldfinch brings you the message to reclaim and reignite your passion and curiosity. Encountering a goldfinch can be an invitation from fairies, pixies, and elves to become more aware of their presence.

Hawk

With single-minded vision, the hawk is a sign to be aware and alert. A hawk brings you the message to let go of limiting beliefs and thoughts in order to attain a higher perspective of self and life. Encountering a hawk is a message to take action on your truth. Be bold and stay on course with what you know is right for you. Spirit guides often get your attention and bring you messages through hawks.

Pigeon

The pigeon brings you the message to hang in there and, if necessary, be stubborn. You can handle whatever comes your way. Don't let your pride get in the way of getting what you want. See the positive within yourself and trust your intuition.

Robin

A robin is a sign of joy, laughter, and new growth. Open your heart and allow the energy of renewal to revitalize you. Robins encourage you to find pleasure in the mundane.

Seagull

Attuned to the earth and to the sea, the seagull brings you the message to integrate your spirituality into your everyday life. Keep your eye on possibilities and on a higher vision of self and life while taking care of daily responsibilities and challenges.

Sparrow

The sparrow is a sign to be industrious, enjoy your friends and other social relationships, and do not underestimate yourself. Power is in small acts of kindness. The sparrow can also bring you the message to be modest. Work toward your goals, but for the time being, allow others to take center stage.

Woodpecker

The woodpecker brings you the message to be yourself and express your own unique style and preferences. Be bold and if making choices and decisions, choose from the heart. The woodpecker can also be a sign that you may need separate from others to explore your true thoughts and feelings.

BUTTERFLY

A butterfly is a positive sign that a loved one on the other side or an angel is with you. Butterflies can also be a sign of transformation and the emergence of your true self after difficulties or healing and renewed health after illness.

CATS

Cats are a sign of intuition, independence, and resistance. If you encounter a cat as a sign this may indicate a need to detach from a current situation and be adaptable. There may also be an air of mystery and the unknown in your present conditions. Listen within, trust your intuitive abilities, and know that goddess energy is guiding you.

Black Cat

A black cat is a sign of mystery and the unknown. If one crosses your path or comes toward you, it is a message to not accept surface explanations and information. Delve deeper and get to the root of current matters. It may also be a sign that someone may be trying to deceive or hide something from you.

Cat Meowing

A meowing cat who is attempting to get your attention is a message to listen within. Use your intuition and trust what feels right in your heart and gut. There is an intuitive message you are meant to hear and trust.

Kitten

A kitten is a message that you are moving toward more independence and individuality. This is a transitionary phase of balancing, taking care of yourself, and allowing others to still support and care for you. Be gentle and encouraging with yourself as your true thoughts and emotions surface and are expressed.

White Cat Crossing Your Path

A white cat crossing your path or coming toward you is a message of healing mind, heart, body, and spirit. Invoke within yourself the energy of love and healing, or seek out a healer who can aid and support you in healing.

A cat of any other color crossing your path is a sign to be true to yourself and take action on what feels right for you. Trust your intuition and do not let others influence you.

CATERPILLAR

A caterpillar is a sign that you are on the right path, positive change and transformation is coming. New life is unfolding from within. Be patient, you are in a process that cannot be rushed.

COW

A cow represents nurturance and the divine mother. A cow is a message to be docile, caring, and allow others to care for you. It may also foretell a coming pregnancy or a successful creative project.

COYOTE

Encountering a coyote is a sign that there is something unknown or hidden in your current situation. Take a step back and be objective. It is not always easy to see our own flaws and limiting patterns. The coyote is coming to you to remind you to be honest and to be careful not to fool yourself. The coyote may also be warning you of someone in your life who is cunning and deceiving.

CRICKET

Seeing a cricket is a sign of introspection and protecting and respecting your innermost thoughts, feelings, and dreams. It is important to understand and accept your sensitivity. Crickets can also be a message to communicate your wants and needs and can be a sign of good luck.

DEER

A sign of feminine energy and independence, deer are a message to be gentle, kind, and compassionate with yourself and others. When you encounter a deer as a sign, its soothing energy brings you a humble and graceful strength that promises fortitude and success.

DOGS

Dogs are a sign of love, devotion, joy, companionship, and forgiveness. When you encounter a dog as a sign, know that you are not alone. They represent the presence of spirit friends and companions who are always with you. Dog energy is connected to the sincere and open heart of love, which asks you to endure the injustices and unfairness of life and keep loving. Don't let anything or anyone lead you away from the center of your most pure inner love.

Growling Dog

A growling or barking dog is a message that you may be misunderstood or betrayed by another. Be sure that it is not you who is betraying yourself or another. It may also be a message that you are not allowing yourself to be vulnerable and open-hearted with others.

Playing Dog

A dog playing in a park or yard alone or with its owner is a sign of success and rejuvenation. Enjoy yourself and have gratitude for the blessings and gifts that have come or are coming your way.

Two dogs playing together is a sign of love, companionship, and joy with another. It can be a message of a coming relationship or friendship or the healing and renewal of a present relationship.

Police Dog

A police dog is a sign of authority and protection. You may need to be alert and aware of others' motives and intent. Expect to be treated well and with dignity.

A police dog can also be a sign that you may need to focus on how you give and express love and affection. You may have co-dependent aspects and character traits that need attention and healing.

Puppy

A puppy is a sign of playfulness and joy. If you have been busy and stressed with work, relationships, or just the daily grind of everyday life, this is a message to adopt a more carefree attitude. Get out of your head, feel your emotions, and have fun. A puppy may also indicate a new friendship or enjoying the company of good friends.

Malnourished

A malnourished-looking stray dog is a sign that you need to develop a more loving attitude toward yourself and those around you. There is a part of you that is suffering and needs attention.

Medium or Large Dog

A medium or larger dog walking on a leash with its owner is a message to share your joy with others and to give to those in need. If you have resentments or anger toward another, or yourself, it is time to practice forgiveness. You have a big heart.

Running Dog

Encountering a dog running loose is a message to examine a situation or relationship and if necessary get away from it to gain better perspective. It may not feel natural or normal to walk away but you need more freedom, even from your own expectations.

Small Dog

A small dog walking on a leash with its owner is a sign that you have within you the qualities and attributes to fulfill your purpose. Don't underestimate what you have to offer others and the world. You have a powerful and loving heart and soul.

Stray Dog

Encountering a stray dog is a message to get in touch with and feel your emotions. If you are feeling lost or confused look within and to those you trust for emotional support. Be careful not to run after empty dreams or relationships. Can also be a sign to give and care for another. Someone in your life might need love and attention.

DRAGONFLY

A dragonfly is a message to explore your thoughts, especially your unconscious, and repressed beliefs and judgments. Let go of repressed negativity so that your light can shine through.

A dragonfly is a spirit messenger who is helping to lift your vibration so that you can more clearly know your purpose and truth. If you see a dragonfly skimming the water's surface, this is a positive sign of prosperity, harmony, and peace.

FISH

Fish are symbolic of emotion, spirituality, and the unconscious. In many spiritual traditions they have deep mystical significance. For instance, in the Christian faith they can represent Christ energy. In the Pagan tradition they can represent the goddess, and in the Celtic belief, they represent wisdom and prophecy.

If you encounter fish as a sign, pay attention. Spirit is sending you the message that despite appearances you are undergoing a spiritual test or initiation of some kind. Listen within and take some time to contemplate your higher purpose.

Carp or Koi

Carp or goldfish bring the message of increase and abundance. They are a sign of the divine presence and a reminder to open your heart and receive blessings. The color of the fish will give you more insight into the message.

Clear Water

If the fish are swimming in clean, clear water, this is a sign of good fortune, deep insights, and the presence of positive spiritual forces.

Dead Fish

Encountering dead fish is a message to let go of negativity, illusionary beliefs, and people who make promises but cannot deliver.

Murky Water

If the water is murky, this is a sign to become better aware of your intent and expectations. Ask yourself what you truly want and desire. Unconscious thoughts and beliefs may be sabotaging what you are experiencing.

People Fishing

Encountering people fishing is a sign that you may be trying to satisfy your deeper soul needs with superficial or empty situations, people, or things. Examine your interests, routines, the people in your life, and how you spend your time, and make changes if your authentic self is not being supported and nourished. May also indicate a deceptive situation or individual.

Flies

Flies buzzing around you is a message to keep things in perspective. Do not let minor annoyances bother and affect you more than they should. Flies may also be a message of quick and rapid change. Stay alert and be responsive and ready to adapt or alter your current plans and expectations.

Fox

Encountering a fox is a message to be alert, use your intelligence, and take swift action. A fox may also be a warning for you to pay attention to shrewd or deceitful people or situations. If you are currently undergoing a difficult situation or condition, the fox is helping you to successfully maneuver your way through it.

Frog

A frog is a message to cleanse and detox and to prepare for positive change and transformation. This could be in the area of health or relationships. They can also signify coming into your power and a sign of good luck for traveling.

Grasshopper

A grasshopper is a sign to take a leap of faith into the unknown. If you have been procrastinating or debating which way to go, the grasshopper is a messenger inspiring you to take a leap of faith. Action will break through the inertia and move you into the current of positive change.

Horse

Horses may be a sign of power, strength, and beauty. If you encounter a horse as a sign it may indicate the need to go forward with a project, new endeavor, or relationship with graceful power and strength. This may be a trying time where you have to be determined but not over-bearing. A horse may also indicate sexual energy and the need to examine and possibly control your passionate desires.

Horse Race

Encountering a horse race is a sign of pride and competition, especially in relationships. Open your heart and feel your feelings. If you are feeling defensive or driven by desire, ask yourself if it is love and harmony that you are looking for, or to win at all costs. Horse racing may also be a message to be financially cautious and may be a warning that this is the not the time to take a risk.

LADYBUG

The ladybug foretells the beginning of a cycle of ease and fulfillment. Worries and stress begin to give way and what you have worked so hard to achieve now comes to you with little effort. Take your time and enjoy this prosperous period.

LIZARD

A lizard is a sign of renewal and creative manifestation. Focus on what is in your heart, not in your head. If you have suffered a loss, it will be made up for in some form. A lizard brings you the power to be your authentic self.

MOTH

A moth is a message to explore your authentic self. If you are not being true to yourself or not allowing others to know the true you, the moth is encouraging you to transform. Look into your heart and let it guide you.

MOOSE

A moose symbolizes solitude, adaptability, and camouflage. If you encounter a moose as a sign it is a message to be patient and humble. The unseen is busy at work behind the scenes. Sometimes it is necessary to build up inner power and energy before going forward. Look for inner beliefs and unconscious motives that may be creating obstacles. A moose can also indicate a visionary and the psychic skill of clairvoyance.

Mouse

A mouse is a sign to lie low and subdue your ego. It may be misleading you and driving your desires. It may also be a sign to come out of the shadows and let yourself be seen.

Possum

Possums are full of energy but like to stay hidden. They are a sign to be inventive, persistent, and protective of your ideas, individuality, and creativity. Now is not the time to seek the spotlight for your achievements.

Rabbit

Seeing a rabbit is a sign of sign of luck, fertility, success, and financial increase. The rabbit can also be a messenger bringing comfort and the emotional assurance that you are not alone.

Rat

Encountering a rat is a message to examine yourself, others, and your current situation for the presence of negative thoughts and emotions. Let go of what no longer serves your highest good and remove yourself from situations and people who erode your self-confidence. Can be a message that you are being deceived.

Snake

A snake is a message to become conscious of your fears, worries, and anxieties and understand how they may be limiting you. Alternatively, snakes are also a sign that through difficulties and challenges you have gained invaluable wisdom.

Squirrel

A squirrel that runs across your path is a sign that you need to slow down and reexamine your goals and desires. You may be wasting your time and energy on a relationship or project that will not give you what you hope for.

Squirrels playing or jumping on trees or wires overhead is a sign to calm your mind through meditation or relaxation. This is a message that your mind may be jumping from one idea or thought to another and you may be unable to hear the quiet inner voice. Breathe and relax.

Chapter 17

Vegetation

The natural world is the original bearer of signs and messages. Throughout the world such things as plants, trees, rocks, the skies, and the weather have been the medium through which the spirit realm has offered guidance and comfort to humanity. Although many signs and messages now also appear through more contemporary things and occurrences, spirit beings still communicate through the natural world.

Berries

Encountering berries on a vine is a message of abundance, prosperity, and plans coming to fruition. Green, unripe berries are a sign to wait and be patient. What you desire is in the formation stage. Berries that are ripe and falling off the vine are a sign to not waste time or procrastinate. Take action on a goal or project and accept an opportunity or invitation.

Cactus

A cactus symbolizes emotional hurt, feeling slighted, or feeling that you have been treated unfairly. It is a message you have the inner resources and love to go it alone if necessary and to heal.

A blooming cactus is a sign of joy and happiness after a period of isolation or difficulties.

CLOVER

Clover is a positive sign of the mystical union of the divine and human realms. It is a message that however mundane your current situation may appear, your soul is working out important karmic issues. Act with pure intent and trust in positive outcomes.

DANDELIONS

Dandelions are a message to be tenacious and determined. There is a refined power within you that is seeking expression.

A white, fluffy dandelion is a message of wishes coming true. Embrace the childlike belief in miracles and allow one to come into your life.

FLOWERS

Flowers are a sign of joy, truth, happiness, and abundance. Flowers, like birds and butterflies, are often divine messages from a loved one on the other side or an angel or spirit guide. The color and type of the flower will reveal more of its message (see *Colors*).

Chrysanthemums

Chrysanthemums are a sign of surprises and the unexpected coming your way. This is a time to shed limiting beliefs and make new discoveries about yourself and the world around you.

Daffodils

Daffodils are a symbol of new love and balancing emotional give-and-take. They can imply giving too much in a relationship or the need to show another how much you care.

Daisies

The daisy is symbolic of purity, innocence, patience, and simplicity. Encountering daisies is a message to draw from these qualities and let go of expectations. Something unexpected is coming your way or will be offered to you that might not initially seem to be what you want or what you are looking for; however, in time you will recognize this as a true gift.

Honeysuckle

Honeysuckle is a sign of magnetism, confidence, and irresistible charm in yourself or in another. It is a message that you have the ability to influence and sway people.

Lavender

A sign of purity, virtue, love, and protection, lavender is a message to let go of negativity and false ideas about yourself and others, and listen to the pure voice of your spirit. Lavender brings you the assurance that grace is at work in your life.

Lilies

Lilies are a sign of rebirth and renewal after challenges and hardships. They are also a symbol of sensitivity and healing ability.

Roses

Roses bring you the message of deep love, romance, and compassion. They can also signify psychic and divination ability. The color of the rose will also reveal more of its meaning.

Sunflowers

A sign of strength and improvement, sunflowers signal the beginning of a prosperous period. Trust your vision of the future and act with faith.

Violets

Violets represent joy and bliss and are a message to become more social and active. This is good time to meet new people.

Waterlilies

A waterlily is a sign of enlightenment, truth, and psychic energy. From the depths of self, your soul is speaking to you. Listen within; your higher self is directing and guiding you.

Withering Flowers

Flowers that are withering and dropping their petals outside of season are a sign of letting go and moving beyond who you believe yourself to be. Aspects of yourself, behaviors, or personality traits that no longer serve you need to be shed.

GARDEN

Encountering a flower garden with many different kinds of flowers is a positive sign of abundance and fulfillment. It is also a message of love from your loved ones on the other side, your angels, and nature spirits.

A vegetable garden is a sign of nourishment and support from nature spirits. It might also be a message of love from a loved one on the other side who enjoyed gardening.

LAWN

Lawns represent the part of ourselves that we show the world and how we interact with others. They can be a message of pride and of social convention.

Dead Grass

A yard with dead grass is a sign of worries, stress, and financial fears. It may be a message to look to a higher power and presence for support and nurturing.

Manicured Lawn

A well-manicured landscaped lawn is a sign of order and respect and attention to detail. It may be a message to express these qualities in your dealings with others. It may also be a message to cultivate and refine the more rebellious and emotionally charged aspects of your personality.

Overgrown

A yard with overgrown weeds is a sign to discern what is important and of value to you and what is not. It may be a message that you are unclear as to your priorities. Be true to yourself and trust what your heart tells you.

Tall Grass

Healthy, tall grass may be a sign of increase, possibly financial, and the ability to influence others. It may also indicate a free spirit and a time of growth.

Moss

Moss is a sign that you may be dependent on something or someone or that someone is overly dependent on you. If you are feeling tired and lack enthusiasm, look at what may be draining your inner resources. Take responsibility for yourself and be careful that you don't try to overdo it and take on too much.

Mushrooms

Mushrooms are a sign of something hidden and unknown. It is a message to be cautious before making a decision. This is not the time to jump in. Take your time as more will soon be revealed.

Rocks

Rocks and boulders are a message of strength, being grounded, and may indicate a solid idea or project. In relationships or career issues, they can be a sign of a strong foundation or steadfast connection.

Smaller stones or pebbles are a sign of the need to put effort into building a solid relationship with another or into a business or enterprise. Small rocks may also indicate proceeding carefully and the possibility of minor issues and irritations.

Trees

Many nature spirits and other spiritual beings inhabit trees. They are pillars that move energy from the deep earth to the skies and back again. Trees are a sign of the full spectrum of life: the past, present, and future. They are the bearers of wisdom and knowledge and the protectors of all living things. A tree can be a message about the individual self, health, and the mind, body, and spirit connection.

Birch

Birch trees are a message to be creative and open to new ways of doing things. Be adaptable and at the same time hold on to your inner vision and goals. The birch can also be a sign that your energy and enthusiasm is contagious. This is the time to trust your actions and move forward.

Evergreen

Evergreen trees are natural conductors of intuitive and psychic energy. They may be a sign from your spirit guides or from nature spirits to listen within and trust your intuitive abilities. Evergreens are also guardians who offer protection and shelter in stressful times. They can be a sign of your need to recharge yourself or to remain on your present course. This is not the time for change.

Falling Tree

A tree falling close by is a sign of transformation and coming change. Nature spirits may be sending you powerful energy from the tree's roots to prepare you for what is to come. Seeing a tree fall naturally is a special gift of power.

Flowering Tree

A flowering tree is a sign of opportunities, new beginnings, and a fresh start to a project, relationship, or career.

A flowering tree whose blossoms have already fallen to the ground is a sign that an opportunity may be passing you by. It is time to take action.

Fruit Tree

Fruit trees with ripe fruit are a sign that your efforts will yield abundance and success.

A fruit tree with rotten fruit is a warning that what looks promising may not yield a positive outcome. Do not be misled by appearances.

If a fruit tree has flowers, it is a message that you are entering a new cycle of substantial change and opportunity.

Group of Trees

A group of trees of the same species is a message of partnerships and group consciousness. Listen to others' knowledge and learn through their experiences. It may also be a message to support others and share your wisdom and knowledge with them.

A natural grove of different varieties of trees and other vegetation is a sign to be yourself and resist the pressure to conform to social norms or other expectations. It may also be a message to allow others to be who they are.

Limb on Ground

A dead tree limb on the ground is a sign of being cut off from and out of touch with your power or your inner truth. This is a message to listen within and trust your thoughts and feelings. While others may have an opinion and try to offer guidance and suggestions, you will not know what is right for you until you feel it from within.

Magnolia

Magnolia trees are a sign of nobility and the ability to confront obstacles with a calm and centered will and determination. Magnolia blossoms or flowers are a sign of beauty and grace, a divine kiss of kindness.

Maple

Maple trees are a sign that someone or something may be coming your way that offers you affection, stimulation, and kindness. It is a message to find and enjoy the sweetness in life.

Oak

Oak trees are a sign of longevity, strength, and practical help. Follow through and devote yourself to existing plans.

Palm

Palm trees are a sign of prosperity and success. They may be a message of a coming promotion or reward of some kind. If the palm tree is growing in a container it is a message to break free of your current situation as your growth and progress is limited.

Single Tree

A single tree represents a single individual or situation. A healthy tree with full foliage is a positive sign of good health, strength, and may be a message to hold your power and express your authentic self. Stand tall and be you.

A single sickly looking tree may indicate an unpromising project or idea and may be a message to take better care of your health.

WEEDS

Weeds and overgrown areas of vegetation are a message to become aware of and root out negative thoughts, criticism, and judgments.

Flowering weeds are a sign of something positive emerging from past difficulties and challenges.

CHAPTER 18

THE SKIES, RAIN, WATER, AND WIND

Signs that come through the skies and the weather are often sent to you from nature spirits and your angels. They are usually of spiritual significance or indicate thoughts, ideas, and communication. Clouds also imply a transitory situation or condition.

Changes in weather that occur while you are actively engaged in a sign oracle exercise are significant. If you previously planned to do an oracle exercise on a specific day, the weather on that day is also a sign or message.

When casting an oracle if you suddenly feel inclined to look up at the sky, pay attention to what you see. Your spirit guides or angels may be trying to get a message to you.

CLEAR AND STILL SKY

A clear sky with no breeze is a sign of inner clarity, wisdom, and a clear mind. It can be a message to trust your intuition and ideas; you are a clear channel for deeper awareness to surface.

CLOUDS

Angels often communicate through clouds. If you notice wispy, white, fluffy clouds, watch how they change and form interesting shapes. The message may be in what you see within the cloud.

Dark Storm Clouds

Dark, stormy clouds are often a sign of setbacks, moodiness, confusion, or not perceiving events or conditions clearly. Conditions may become more intense before they are resolved.

Dense Solid Clouds

A dense cloud covering is a sign of fixed thoughts, judgments, and ideas. It is a message to open your mind to possibilities and let go of your expectations. Sometimes we need to walk away from a problem to receive the solution. Your intuition will get you further than logic and reasoning.

Grey Clouds

Grey clouds can indicate mental chatter, doubt, or confusion. This may be a message to be patient. Whatever is causing confusion is temporary and will pass.

Small Cloud

A small cloud covering the sun is a sign that the difficulties or challenges that you may be experiencing are temporary.

Sun Peeking through White Clouds

The sun peeking in an out of clouds can indicate new ideas, increased knowledge, and divine wisdom. Confusion and uncertainty is temporary and will soon dissipate.

Sun through Dark Clouds

The sun breaking through dense, dark clouds, is a sign of a positive breakthrough in what may appear to be a dismal or confusing situation. Your angels and loved ones on the other side are watching over you. A sign of joy and coming happiness.

White Clouds

White, large clouds with a spattering of grey clouds indicate thoughts, ideas, and insight. This may be a message to recognize and distinguish between higher thoughts and thoughts that are generated from the ego and from fear. Focus on the thoughts that induce feelings of expansion and inspiration.

FOG

Fog is a sign of the unknown, confusion, and lack of focus. Someone is not being honest or is hiding important information from you. It might also indicate that you are in denial and not accepting the truth about someone or something. Sometimes we become confused and do not know which direction to take; the fog is a sign to slow down and wait for clarity before making a decision.

JET TRAIL

Seeing a white, long, straight-line jet trail is a sign of spiritual activity and an affirmation from the spirit realm that you are being guided and led. A jet trail asks you to lift your consciousness and remember that even though you are in a physical body, you can commune with higher levels of wisdom. However, remember that you must come back down to earth and share what you receive.

MOON

The moon is a sign of feminine energy, mystery, intuition, and emotion, and is often associated with the goddess. The moon brings insight into the depths of the unconscious and our soul awareness. It may also indicate the possibility of deception and the surfacing of the shadow side of our or someone's personality.

Crescent Moon

If there is a crescent moon in the sky while you are casting an oracle, this is a sign to be cautious and to not take on new projects or take chances. In relationships, balance your emotions and be kind and forgiving. In this way you can increase intimacy and come to a better understanding of another and of yourself.

Crescent Moon and One Close Star

If there is a crescent moon and a close star in the sky while you are casting the oracle, it is a sign of spiritual attainment and good fortune. Pay attention to new ideas and chance encounters with others or opportunities that come your way. This can also be an indication that you're going through a spiritual transformation.

Full Moon

A full moon is a sign to express your feminine energy, intuition, and creativity. It a message to feel the depths of your emotions and soulful desires, and allow the mystery and power of the divine mother to heal you.

Moon and Clouds

The moon breaking through clouds is a sign of increasing intuitive awareness and the emergence of healing abilities. It may also announce a coming pregnancy, or spiritual rebirth and renewal.

Sun and Moon

Seeing the moon when the sun is in the sky is symbolic of the balance between male and female energy, and conscious and unconscious awareness. It can be a message to delve into the unconscious and allow any repressed emotions to surface. It can also point to the need to bring balance to your own male and female energy.

RAIN

Rain indicates emotional and spiritual cleansing and clearing. It can also be a symbol of prosperity, abundance, and love coming your way.

Drizzle

Drizzle or mist is a positive sign of gentle spiritual nurturing and inner peace. It may be a message to meditate, spend time alone in contemplation, and listen within.

Heavy Downpour

A sudden, heavy downpour is a message to open your heart, let go of past emotional wounds, forgive yourself and others, and prepare to receive. Abundance, prosperity, and new love are coming your way.

Sun Shower

A sun shower is a special divine blessing. Your prayers are heard and being answered.

Steady Rain

A long, steady rain and dreary sky is a sign of a surge of emotions. Many illnesses and depression have their roots in unacknowledged and suppressed emotions. Feel and express your feelings, even the uncomfortable ones, in a safe and supportive environment. This is a time of deep emotional clearing and detoxing.

RAINBOW

A sign from ascended masters and angels of coming joy, abundance, hope, and fulfillment. Rainbows also bring the message of a happy family and could indicate a coming marriage or pregnancy.

SLEET OR ICE

Sleet is a sign to be cautious and careful. It is not the time to move forward with a plan or enterprise. It may also be a message that your true feelings may be frozen and suppressed. Take some time to allow your emotions to surface and to become aware of them.

SNOW

Falling snow is a sign from nature spirits and angels, reminding you of the magic of life. It may indicate the need for solitude, inner peace, and time away from stress and worries. Alternatively, it may also indicate something hidden or unknown; be patient and wait before taking action.

Snow in Sunlight

Snow falling in the sunlight or the sun shining on the snow may be a message that you are undergoing a purifying and spiritual healing.

STAR

Seeing a star during the day is a sign to be true to what inspires you and to follow your heart, no matter how impractical or nonlogical it may seem.

A falling star is a sign of hope, optimism, and a message that a wish or blessing is being fulfilled

Seeing a meteor shower is a sign of divine, angelic, and higher-self activity. Change and transformation is taking place and will soon manifest. This is a message letting you know that you are seen and loved. The spirit realm is showering you with love.

STORMS

A sudden storm or thunder and lightning foretells the breaking up of existing tension and may be a message that you need to release emotional stress, frustration, or anger in a healthy way. Although storms are a message of unstable and changing conditions, they may indicate positive improvement and renewal.

SUN

The sun symbolizes male energy, activity, assertiveness, happiness, and extroversion. The sun is a sign if you notice anything unusual connected with it.

Clouds Covering Sun

Clouds covering the sun is a sign that the difficulties or hardships that you are going through are temporary. There is light behind the darkness. It may also suggest that future plans or desires may not manifest in the way that you hope for. It may also indicate that you are blocking your own light from shining.

Sun Rays

Being able to visually see the sun's rays and the spectrum of light within them is a sign of spiritual illumination and psychic abilities. If you encounter this as a sign, it indicates that you have gifts to give to others and to the world. You will have increasing influence with others and in the public. It can also indicate that your perception is clear, and to trust your intuition.

WATER

Water is highly symbolic and often used by the spirit realm to convey messages about love, emotions, prosperity, and spirituality. The form and purity of the water you encounter will give you clues as to its significance.

Floods

Floods are a sign that you are being swept away by cultural norms and societal expectations. You are losing touch with your authentic feelings and sense of self. It is time to listen within to your personal truth.

Fountain

Encountering a fountain with clear water is a positive sign. There is good reason why people throw coins into fountains while making a wish. They are a magical sign of fulfillment and blessings coming your way.

A fountain with no water or water that is stagnant and murky symbolizes feelings of emptiness and the need to renew yourself emotionally and spiritually. It may also indicate financial lack or loss.

Ice

Ice on your path is a sign of frozen emotions and a hardened heart. However difficult they may be, allow conditions to soften you. Listen within and accept all that you are experiencing and feeling. Let yourself feel.

Irrigation Ditch

An irrigation ditch is a message to further develop your intuitive ability to channel and communicate with the spirit realm. It may be a sign of coming abundance and positive outcomes. It might indicate your ability or your need to channel your emotions in positive ways. If you are feeling uncentered or unsure, an irrigation ditch is a sign to focus your energy and reign in your emotions.

Mud

Mud or muddy water is a sign of confusion, indecision, and procrastination. It is a message that even though you may not be sure of what to do or how to proceed, take some form of action. Move forward in some way, even if you lack confidence, and clarity will follow.

Pond

A tranquil pond or lake is a sign to avoid overreaching. This is not the time to make plans or focus on the future. Success will come as you stay in present time and attend to what is happening right now. A pond can also be a calming message to be still and listen within.

A pond or lake that has choppy or dark muddy water is symbolic of minor irritations and frustration. It is a message to not allow problems or issues to overwhelm you. What you are experiencing is only temporary. It may also be a message to keep your expectations reasonable. Change is coming and bringing improvement and clarity.

A recreational lake with boats and/or people swimming can be a message to enjoy and have fun with others. It may also signify satisfying spiritual and emotional interactions with others and companionship.

Pool

A pool with people enjoying themselves is a sign that success will come as you socialize and network. It may also be an indication of increasing and positive emotional connections with others.

If the pool is empty, it is a message that your emotional life may be out of balance, especially as it relates to friends and family.

A pool full of children is a message to get in touch with your child-like nature, innocence, sense of wonder, and curiosity. Approach others and your present conditions with an uncomplicated and nonjudgemental attitude. A sign of spiritual rebirth and renewal, open your heart and mind and see with fresh eyes.

A lap pool is a sign of contemplation and meditation and the need for quiet time in reflection.

Puddle

A puddle is a message to pay attention to your communication with those close to you. In doing this you will keep potential problems, especially relationship issues, small and manageable.

Reservoir

A reservoir is a sign of purity, vitality, and the ability to nurture and be of service. The divine is flowing through you, so that you can be a source of healing to others.

River

Encountering a swift moving, clear river is a sign of making progress and a suggestion from the spirit realm to go with the current. This is not the time to be stubborn, overly individualistic, or try to get your way.

A slow moving, muddy, or dark river is a sign that you may be over-compromising in some area of your life. It is a message that going along with others' plans and desires will not get you what you want.

Stream

A stream is a sign to trust your instincts and intuition. This is a message that success and abundance will come as you listen within. It also indicates that you are on track; keep going forward as your ideas, plans, and new projects or relationships will continue to grow and expand.

Tower

A water tower may be a sign of higher spiritual forces that you can draw spiritual guidance from. It may also indicate spiritual or emotional insight and help that you can offer others. You have more wisdom and strength to draw from than you may know.

WATERFALL

A waterfall is a message of coming change that may feel tumultuous and out of your control. It may indicate that you are experiencing a karmic situation or condition that does not make sense or one that you feel powerless to resolve. Release and let go; calmer times will follow.

Alternatively, a waterfall may also indicate a powerful spiritual and emotional healing is or is about to take place.

WIND

The wind is a sign of an increase in energy, new ideas, and may be a push from spirit to move forward or take action. It may also indicate our thoughts and our ability to go with the flow.

Gentle Wind

A gentle wind is a touch from the spirit realm. Someone or a loving higher power is reaching out to you. If you have been stressed or rushing about this is a message that all is in order. Take your time and have gratitude for the positive.

Strong Wind

A sudden strong wind suggests new ideas and innovative thoughts. It may also be a sign that it is time to let go of something and be open to a new way of thinking.

Walking against Wind

If you are walking against the wind, this is a sign of possible resistance and going against the current. If you are trying to make something happen, this can be a message to explore another direction.

Walking with Wind

Walking with the wind at your back suggests divine support and possibly the support of others. You are on track and going with the flow of your higher self.

Wind Gusts

Wind gusts suggest that your thinking may be scattered and you may need to focus your ideas and thoughts. Wind gusts may also be a message to pay attention to intuitive insights.

CHAPTER 19

NUMBERS

You likely will notice many numbers on homes, buildings, street signs, license plates, and other signs, structures, and vehicles. Not all of the numbers you see are signs and messages. Recurring numbers, number synchronicities, or numbers that have personal significance to you are significant. Numbers contain important messages and may also confirm and support other signs and messages. For instance, a significant number on a building or on a license plate can be a sign that the building or car is a sign.

0

Zero is a sign of wholeness, completion, nonphysical energy, and indicates the presence of spirit. If you encounter a 0 as a sign, it is important to listen within for guidance and the voice of spiritual presence. This is a sign of unity with all of life and elevates you to a higher wisdom and awareness. Alternatively, it can signify going back to the beginning and letting go of what you desire and what you have been trying to make happen.

1

A sign of the leader, the number 1 is a message of new beginnings, going it on your own, and taking action. If you encounter a 1, you have the presence and power of clarity and clear awareness. Trust yourself, and if need be, separate yourself from group consciousness and thinking. Be original and authentic.

2

The number 2 is a message that the focus is on relationships, harmony, duality, and partnership, and may be a sign of competition. If you encounter the number 2 as a sign, it may indicate that it is important to give of yourself to others or to something that you believe in. A number of coupling, it also may be a message of a coming relationship or a healing or an improvement in a relationship.

3

The number 3 is a sign of coming joy, success, creativity, and connection to the spirit realm. Three is a spiritual number in that it highlights the trinity. Mother, Crone, Maiden; father God, son, and holy spirit; and mind, body, spirit, are three example of the divine trinity. The number 3 may also indicate the need to unite with those of like mind and can be a message to join with others, but be careful not to form separate and exclusive relationships.

4

The number 4 is a sign of the need for stability, becoming centered, and being practical. Encountering a number 4 as a sign can indicate the manifestation of an idea, project, or desire. The number of the formless becoming form, it is a powerful number if you wish to see something come into fruition. It is also a sign of stability and strengthening of a current project or for something already in manifest form. The number 4 is in many ways a pat on the back from the spirit world, letting you know that your imaginative powers and physical application is bringing success.

5

The number 5 is a sign of present or upcoming unpredictability, change, and the need for adaptability and a new perspective. If you encounter the number 5 as a sign, it is important to pay attention to your thoughts and actions. This is a time of change and fluctuation, and the outcome is dependent on how you confront the current conditions and proceed. Take time to listen within and go forward one step at a time.

6

The number 6 is a message to practice compassion and forgiveness with yourself and others. Encountering a 6 as a sign is a message to be aware of others' needs and communicate with patience and understanding. The number 6 indicates that you are at the turning point of a significant shift. You are about to step into something new. Take a look back and bless all that has supported your journey.

7

The number 7 is a message of the hidden and unknown. If you encounter a number 7 as a sign, it is important to take time for yourself in solitude and introspection. 7 supports intuition, wisdom, and can reveal information that you have not been aware of. 7 also highlights the need to be careful to not mistake illusion for reality. When the number 7 is present, you are deepening your soul wisdom with new insights and new awareness.

8

The number 8 is a message of achievement and success through application and power from within. When you encounter the number 8 as a sign, the issue is power in some form. It is up to you how to proceed. The energy of the 8 encourages you to draw from the higher spiritual forces and use power wisely and for good. Eight can also signify coming success in the areas of business and finance.

9

The number 9 is a sign of attainment, accomplishment, and the ability to influence others. If you encounter the number 9 as a sign, your current magnetism is drawing others to you. The divine may be channeling love and wisdom through you for the betterment of others. Practice altruism and express your passion. The number 9 is drawing something to closure and bringing you further into the spotlight and increasing your effectiveness in the world.

10

The number 10 can be interpreted as a number 1 (1 + 0 = 1). It can also be taken as a 10, which is a number of completion and a sign that a new beginning is on the way. If you encounter a clear number 10, pay attention to detail and complete any projects and take action on something that you have wanted to do. If you have been procrastinating, 10 is telling you to complete the cycle and celebrate.

NUMBER COMBINATIONS

Number combinations are interpreted by combining the digits until you reach a single digit.

For instance, 378 equals 3 + 7 + 8 = 18 then 1+ 8 = 9. However, 18 can also be a sign of both the number 1 and the number 8. Use your intuition, past personal association with the number, and other confirming signs to discern the interpretation method.

For example, the number 78 is of personal significance for me. It is a positive symbol of my connection with my daughter. I have come to this interpretation after many years of experiencing synchronicities related to this number and my daughter. The number 36 has no personal meaning for me. If it frequently appears I would interpret it as the number 9, as 3 + 6 = 9.

REPEATING SAME DIGITS

When you notice the same number recurring, it can be interpreted as a very potent aspect of the single digit number or a higher vibration portal.

The numbers 11 and 22 are especially significant as they are master numbers.

11

The number 11 is a message from your angels inviting you into a higher divine angelic vibration. Many people who are on a spiritual path and

opening to an increase in connection with the spirit realm begin to encounter the number 11 or a combination of this number, 1:11 or 11:11.
If you encounter this number as a sign, the gates of spirit are opening for
you.

22

The number 22 is a sign of power and indicates that you are working
in unison with the divine forces to manifest and create on the earthly
realm. If your question or concerns have to do with a relationship, the
number 22 is an auspicious and positive sign. It indicates that it is important to form and focus on a spiritual connection with another or
that a soul mate is coming into your life. In other areas, the number 22
is a sign of strength and the manifestation of your dreams. It is the
master builder number.

33

The number 33 is a sign of compassion, healing, and the ability to teach
and uplift others.

44

The number 44 is a sign of creating stability and opportunities for others. It can point to a business or enterprise that will benefit many.

55

The number 55 is a sign of changes and possible confusion. Look within
and listen to your intuition. Trust yourself and be aware of how your
choices affect others.

66

The number 66 is a sign that divine wisdom and love is seeking to work
through you. This is a calling into divine service.

77

The number 77 is a sign of the mystic and rapid awakening. It is a separating of paths and leaving worldly consciousness for the inner solitude of spiritual ascension.

88

The number 88 is a message to be assertive, authentic, and confidently walk your most true path. In doing so you pave the way for others.

99

The number 99 is a sign of the visionary and the assurance that you have the ability to inspire and enlighten others. It can also be a caution to not be too idealistic and expect too much from others.

CHAPTER 20

COLORS

You will notice and see many different colors while actively participating in the Living Oracle. Not every color that you see is significant and should be interpreted. Colors that are signs and contain messages will likely appear in patterns or through synchronicity. They will reinforce and confirm other signs and messages.

For instance, seeing a silver car is not necessarily significant. However, seeing three or more silver cars one after the other is likely a sign. It may indicate that both the color and the cars are significant. Colors can give more information about other signs. For instance, the color of a dog or cat will help you to interpret its message. In the same way, the color of other signs should be considered when interpreting them.

BLACK

Like most colors, black can be either positive or negative. It can be a message of stability, power, or hidden potential. If you encounter the color black, this may also be a protective sign. Because black absorbs negativity and hides energy, this may be a warning to stay the course and be aware of what is going on in your environment. Black is a solid vibration that may help stabilize you after change or upheaval. Keep in mind that black may also be a sign of dark forces, danger, or despair, so be cautious and trust your gut feelings and intuition about others and situations.

BLUE

The color blue is a sign of peace, truth, and tranquility. If you encounter blue as a sign, it is offering you the assurance that peaceful times are ahead. You can relax and know that everything is in order. The color blue also promotes reconciliation and positive communication. Express your needs and desires to others and listen to what others have to share with you. However, be careful not to be too idealistic and indulgent.

Darker blues may indicate depression or feeling down. Light blues can be a message of hopeful new beginnings, new life, or a fresh start.

BROWN

Brown is associated with nature spirits, the earth, and practicality. If you encounter brown as a sign, it is a message to connect with nature, trust your instincts, and stay balanced in the here and now. Brown as a vibration is humble and hardworking. It does not seek recognition or to be in the spotlight. It may be an indication to stay focused on your goals and to do good for its own reward. This is not the time to take changes or to seek idealistic aspirations. This is the *what you see is what you get* color.

Too much brown or muddy dull brown can indicate confusion, lack of clarity, and laziness or being stuck.

GOLD

The color gold is a message of prosperity, success, and prestige. Encountering gold as a sign indicates the attainment of higher ideas and positive connections with others. Gold can be a sign that gifts, both spiritual and material, may be coming your way. The vibration of gold is warm and inviting. It is an indication that in some way you have or will soon arrive at a place of contentment and enjoyment. Soak it in and be open to what comes your way.

GREEN

Green is a color of healing, fertility, new growth, and renewal after trauma or difficulties. If you encounter green as a sign it indicates that healing forces are present. This may be a sign of your ability to heal others and a gentle nudge to awaken the dormant healing energy within you. It may also be an indication that you are in a situation that needs healing and restoration. The color green offers you the vibration of sanctuary, restfulness, and the confirmation that you are being watched over.

Florescent or bright greens may be a sign of jealousy or envy.

ORANGE

Orange is a stimulating color that brings with it the message of friendship, vitality, and personal warmth. It is associated with the sun and with optimism and enjoyment. If you encounter the color orange as a sign, it indicates the need to get out of your current routine and adopt a positive perspective. Orange is a vibration that instills energy and connection with others. It may be a message to share your gifts with others and to offer your services or talents to the public. Orange is also symbolic of gut intuition and may be indicating the need to listen to your gut awareness and knowing.

A dull orange or shadowy orange may indicate pessimism or an overly impulsive tendency. Adventure is good, but make sure you are grounded.

PINK

Connected to the angelic realm, the color pink is representative of new love, compassion, kindness, and unconditional love. If you encounter pink as a sign it may be a message from the angels letting you know that they are near. A vibration of empathy and sensitivity, pink highlights the need to protect yourself from the harshness of negativity, toxins, and people or situations that may cause you stress or drain your resources. Pink vibration is a soothing energy that asks you to nurture your deepest needs and to offer this nurturing to others.

PURPLE

The color purple represents royal and higher thoughts, spiritual attainment, and inner riches. If you encounter the color purple as a sign it is a message that your intuitive and psychic abilities are increasing and that you can place more trust in them. When you encounter purple, it is likely a message from your spirit guides acknowledging your intuitive strengths and offering you their assistance. It may also indicate the opening of your third eye and clairvoyant abilities. The vibration of purple is spiritually stimulating and may be a suggestion to pay attention to your dreams and to use your imagination to reinforce your deepest desires.

RED

The color red can be a message of creativity, passion, empowerment and assertiveness or a warning to subdue your anger or passion. It may also be a sign to stop before going ahead with a project, relationship, or venture. If you encounter the color red as a sign, it indicates action in some form needs to be taken. Because red can be a quick-changing and unpredictable energy, be aware of your motives and intent before going forward. Red also represents love; this may be romantic or love in a higher vibration. Use love in its most pure form.

Too much red or deep blood red can indicate anger or aggressiveness in yourself, a situation, or another.

SILVER

The color silver is associated with the moon and feminine energy. When you encounter the color silver as a sign it indicates the need to focus on your feminine energy and explore metaphysics and spirituality. Silver is a vibration that gently illuminates and helps us to notice more and to be conscious of those things that we may have been in denial about or repressing. A vibration of detoxing, cleansing, and clearing, silver as a sign may be a suggestion to take some time to let go of negative habits, limited thoughts, and to detox the physical body.

Silver is a protective spiritual energy that promotes solitude and inner reflection.

TURQUOISE

The color turquoise is symbolic of calm, concentration, mental clarity, and balance. If you encounter turquoise as a sign, it indicates that it is important to approach your current situation or question with objectivity and a bit of detachment. Its vibration reduces anxiety and promotes open conversation without ego. Because turquoise can bring balance to intensity and emotional stress, it may be a sign to take some time away from current stresses and restore your inner clarity. Turquoise may also be a sign that you may be sought after to give advice to others or participate in public speaking.

Too much or bright turquoise may indicate secrets and deception or a lack of emotional connection with someone.

WHITE

The color white is associated with the divine and with pureness, clarity, innocence, and new beginnings. If you encounter the color white as a sign, it is time to perceive the truth. Too often we only see what we want and are overly focused on our needs. The vibration of white lifts your perception to a higher level. It asks you to become aware of your oneness with all of life and to have compassion for others and put aside selfishness and completion. It may indicate that your soul and spirit are ready to lead you to a higher vision of yourself and to real and everlasting joy. It is time to wipe the slate clean and make choices from your divine inner knowing.

Too much white can indicate a lack of passion, desire, and energy to maintain a project, relationship, or new venture.

YELLOW

The color yellow is associated with happiness, energy, intellect, and mental stimulation. If you encounter the color yellow as a sign, it may be motivating you to new ideas and a message to analyze your situation. The vibration of yellow sharpens your thoughts and supplies the energy to be mentally active and engaged. At times it can be overstimulating, and encountering an abundance of yellow may be a sign that you are overthinking your current situation. You may need to clear your mind and meditate. Yellow is a fast vibration that can provide energy and stimulation to move forward on a project or undertaking. It is a sign to think things through, and it empowers you to come to a deeper knowing and truth.

Bright yellow or an overabundance of yellow may also be a message of betrayal, deceit, and indecisiveness.

Violet

The color violet is associated with creativity, imagination, and originality. If you encounter violet as a sign it is a message to pursue your individuality and to take chances with your creativity. Often a sign from ascended masters, violet lets you know that your efforts to perceive the beauty in life and within yourself and others is being supported and encouraged. It is through your creativity that you will be able to inspire and be a light to others. Violet is a high-vibration color that sparks the awareness of your higher purpose and promotes communication and connection with divine presence. It is a message of oneness and brings with it the message that *all is well*.

Too much violet can indicate that your current plans, a relationship, or endeavor is impractical. It may be that you need to ground your ideas to achieve what you desire.

CHAPTER 21

ACTIONS AND ACTIVITY

The actions and activities that you encounter while casting the Living Oracle can be important signs and messages. Pay attention to what is happening around you, and don't discount its importance. Use your gut feelings and intuition to discern what actions and activities are significant.

AFFECTIONATE COUPLE

People walking hand-in-hand, kissing, or hugging is a sign of relationship harmony and increasing feelings of love and connection with others. It may also foretell a new partnership or love interest entering your life.

ARGUING

Encountering people arguing can be a sign of conflict, disagreement, and the need to be more aware of your communication with others. It can also be a sign of repressed anger and inwardly focused feelings of discontent and conflict.

BOY PLAYING

Seeing a boy playing alone is a sign that growth is taking place in your life in ways that may not be obvious. There may be a current situation where you need to take action or be assertive. Confront issues head-on. Seeing a boy playing may also be a sign that there is a male in your life who may not be acting responsibly and is not dependable.

Car Problems

Seeing a broken-down car on the side of the road is a message to slow down and assess your mental, emotional, and physical well-being and health. There may be an unknown problem or issue that needs your attention.

Seeing someone changing a flat tire is a sign to reach out and allow another to assist you in some way. This may be a health practitioner or therapist of some kind; you are low on energy and need assistance.

Carrying Bags or Luggage

Encountering people who are carrying bags or luggage is a sign of feeling weighed down by responsibilities, worries, or fears. This is a message to lighten your load and let go of what is holding you back from moving forward.

Children Playing

Children playing can be a sign of happiness, innocence, and a message to adopt a carefree attitude. It may also be a message to reclaim an aspect of yourself from the past that may have been forgotten or left behind. This may be a personal truth, a belief in what is possible, or your innocence.

Dancing

Encountering people dancing is a sign to loosen up and release stress and tension in the body and feel joy. You do not need to dance, but do something that brings you pleasure. Dancing can also be a message to allow your spirit and heart to lead you. If you have been holding back or approaching life in a more logical and rational way, people dancing is a suggestion to let go, feel the joy of life, and trust your heart.

Delivery

Seeing a delivery being made is a sign of communication or action, or it may be a message that a gift is coming your way. The type of delivery may give you a clue as to the area of focus. (See *Transportation*.)

DIRECTING TRAFFIC

Police directing traffic is a sign that current conditions are out of our control. There is someone or something outside of yourself that is influencing your progress and what you are experiencing. Wait and be patient; this is only temporary. You may need the help of an expert or professional to sort things out.

DIRECTIONS

Being asked for directions is a message to share your gifts with others. This may be something or in an area that you do not necessarily realize can be helpful or useful to others. This is a sign that others may need something from you, perhaps a skill, advice, or love.

FAMILY WITH BABY STROLLER

Seeing a family with a baby stroller is a sign of coming change that will bring with it a sense of renewal and rebirth. If present circumstances do not appear to be positive or if you have become frustrated by a lack of progress, seek out others who are supportive and can be helpful.

GIRL PLAYING

A girl playing by herself is a message to be aware of your emotional vulnerability and to take care of yourself. Sometimes we want to trust and open up to others who may not be reliable. Share your feelings with those who are nurturing and safe.

JOGGERS

Encountering people running or jogging is a sign of steady movement toward a goal. You may need to work hard, be organized, and apply yourself. It might also be a message to take action in some area of your life where your fears have been holding you back.

If people are running or jogging in opposite directions it may be a sign that an inner conflict may need to be resolved in order to reach your goals. If you seem to be confused or not sure of what you want, look deeper, there may be unacknowledged feelings or desires.

LANDSCAPING CREW

Encountering a crew of landscapers is a sign of managing and improving your personal desires and impulses. If large equipment is involved, it could be a message that you may need the assistance of others to transform and change.

Encountering landscapers installing a pool or adding a water feature or fountain is a message to work with the divine creative forces to express your authentic self and share it with others.

PERSON HOLDING BABY

Encountering someone holding a baby is a sign of a new idea, project, desire, or wish coming to fruition. However, what this is may not be initially obvious or seem significant. It is important to pay attention to the opportunities that come your way.

A woman holding a baby is a message that you need to nurture and support new creative ideas and possibilities. It may also indicate that there are others who need your emotional support.

A man holding a baby is a message to go forward with outer goals, aspirations, and ambitions. This may be a message that it is time to act on your dreams.

MOVING TRAIN

Encountering a train that is moving in the direction you are going is a sign of coming support and making progress.

If the train is moving in the opposite direction than you are moving, it is a sign that you are going against the current. You may have an uphill or difficult struggle ahead.

Walking under a bridge with a moving train on it is a positive sign that higher benevolent energies are guiding you. Release your personal desires and motivations and allow yourself to be led.

PERSON SITTING ALONE

Seeing someone sitting alone is a sign of contemplation, introspection, solitude, and meditation. It may be a message that you need quiet and alone time. It may be time to go it alone.

PREGNANT WOMAN

Encountering a pregnant woman is a message that a new opportunity, desire, relationship, goal, or project has recently come into your life or is about to. Be sure to nurture your creativity and be open to possibilities. Be patient; even if you do not see it coming, a new beginning is on its way.

RACE, RUNNING, BIKING

Encountering a running or biking competition or other type of race is a sign that you may feel as if you are being tested or pushed to your limit in some area. It is a message that with strength of mind and heart you will succeed.

ROAD BEING PAVED

A road being paved is a positive sign of a new beginning unfolding and easy progress to come. It may also indicate that you may need to examine the path you are on and make improvements or pave a new way for yourself.

ROADWORK

Encountering roadwork is a sign of an obstruction or hurdle impeding your current path. This is likely an external or outer force or situation that you may have to maneuver around. It also indicates that there are benevolent forces helping to resolve any obstacles.

SKATEBOARD, SKATES

Encountering children or adults on skateboards or skates is a sign of creativity and unconventionality. You are in a unique position of ease and expansion. Trust the momentum that you have achieved. This is a message that taking a risk will likely pay off in a positive way.

Ice Skates

Encountering others ice skating is a sign to be objective and careful. Not everything is what it may seem to be. This may also be a sign to open your heart and feel your feelings and emotions. If you have been feeling depressed or stuck, allow your feelings to surface.

SPORTS

Encountering people playing basketball, tennis, football, or another sport indicates friendly competition and group effort. It may be a sign to *get in the game* and participate in life. Now is not the time to stand by and wait. This is a message of jumping into a project or opportunity, or to make a choice and apply effort to making something work.

STUNG BY A BEE, WASP, OR HORNET

If you are stung by a bee, wasp, or hornet, this is a message to become aware of any inner frustration, pain, or anger. The sting is meant to bring it to the surface, where you can express and release it. In this way it is a bit of a gift. A sting may also be a sign that you will or already have had an encounter with a critical, selfish, or overly defensive person.

STREET BEGGING

Encountering someone who is asking for money is a message to examine your self-worth and your thoughts, beliefs, and feelings surrounding money and generosity. It is always a good idea to express generosity when confronted with someone who is lacking or suffering. What we give others, we give to ourselves. When you encounter someone asking for money, your spirit guides and angels may be encouraging you to open your heart and express the law of abundance.

STREET VENDOR

A street vendor is a sign that your needs will be met in unexpected and unconventional ways. It is a message to let go of your expectations and be willing to receive goodness into your life, however it arrives.

If the street vendor is selling food, it is a sign to explore unconventional avenues for improving your health.

TRAFFIC ACCIDENT

Witnessing a traffic accident is a sign of danger and a warning to be cautious. There are forces and influences that you may not suspect could be harmful. It may also be a sign to extend help to others.

TRAFFIC JAM

A traffic jam is a sign of feeling stuck with no options and being prevented from moving forward by outer influences. It is a message to be patient and wait. This may also indicate that you may need to get out of the box and be original and creative.

WORKERS IN A PUBLIC SPACE

Encountering a crew of workers in a public place is a sign that you may need help, guidance, and support from others to move forward in fulfilling your career goals and life purpose. It may indicate coming opportunities to influence others in a public forum. Workers may also be a sign to assist others in helping them to build their dreams.

WORKERS IN A SEWER

Work being done underground or in a sewer is a sign that something in the past or something you have left behind needs to be revisited and let go of. This is a message that there are negative or toxic thoughts, feelings, and experiences that are influencing your current situation. You may need expert help in getting to the root source and releasing what is no longer serving your highest good.

WORKERS IN A SUBWAY

Workers in a subway or subway tunnel is a sign that others' thoughts, feelings, and beliefs are influencing you on an unconscious level. Take your time in becoming more aware of what is right and good for you. As you do this, you make steady progress toward your goals.

WORKERS ON A TELEPHONE POLE

Work being done on cable or telephone poles is a sign of communication and the ability to understand and engage with others. This is a message that you have the innate ability to influence and impact others. It may be a message to reach out and expand your friendships or increase networking opportunities. If you have been wondering whether to contact someone, this is a *yes* sign.

YARD WORK

People doing yard work, gardening, or farming is a message to take action and root out negativity and habits that are not supporting your higher aims and desires.

Seeing people mowing a lawn is a sign to take some time to organize your thoughts and feelings and decide on a course of action. Be aware of others' expectations, but choose what ultimately is right for you.

CHAPTER 22

SMELLS AND SOUNDS

Not all smells and sounds are significant. Those that stand out and that persist may be a sign.

SMELLS

Burning

The smell of something burning is a sign of the beginning of a new path. Forces are clearing the way for a fresh start; you cannot go back to the old ways. Smells of burning may also be a warning to not push to try to make something happen. Practice patience.

Food

Food smells are a sign that the spirit realm is offering you nurturance and love. Open your heart and allow yourself to be cared for.

Garbage

The smell of garbage is a sign that you need to let go of something or someone. This may be a desire, an expectation, or another person. Something has outlived its usefulness. It may also be a message to question others' motives and possibly your own.

Pleasant

If there is a pleasant scent in the air from no known source, it is a sign that the heavens and divine presence are watching over you.

SOUNDS

Arguing

Hearing arguing or fighting can suggest an inner conflict or indecisiveness. It can be a message to pay attention to your self-talk and to be kind and accept yourself for who you are. If there is an inner struggle or battle that you are experiencing, acknowledge it and focus on loving yourself and being compassionate instead. As you do this, new insights and awareness will surface.

Bands

Hearing live music from a band is a sign to express your emotions and your true self. The world needs to hear what you have to say. If you like the music this can be a sign to relax and enjoy yourself and others.

Birds

Hearing birds singing is a message from the higher spheres of love and divine presence. It is a sign of coming happiness.

Car Alarm

Hearing the sound of a car alarm can be a message to stay on your path and stick to your goals. Trust that you know what is right for you. There may be someone or a condition that may be trying to deter or hijack your plans or aspirations.

Cheering

Hearing people cheering is a sign of accomplishment and coming success. If nothing comes to mind, you may have achieved a goal or learned a soul lesson. In some way you are a winner. Imagine all of your loved ones on the other side, your angels, and your spirit guides sending you joyous applause.

Crickets

Hearing crickets is a sign of good luck. Listen within to your inner voice, your angels, loved ones on the other side, and spirit guides. You will be lead to an opportunity to increase abundance, love, and joy.

Crying or Screaming Child

Hearing a crying or screaming child is a sign of pent-up emotional stress, frustration, and the need to feel nurtured and cared for on a deep level. Treat yourself lovingly and compassionately. There is a child within you that needs your love and care.

Fire, Police, Ambulance

Hearing the siren of an emergency vehicle is a sign to take immediate action in a current condition or situation. Sometimes doing something, even if you are not sure it is the correct action, creates momentum and the opportunity for spirit to step in and bring healing and improvement.

Laughter

If you hear laughter, it is likely someone in the spirit realm reminding you not to take things too seriously. The spirit realm loves to laugh. Loosen up and enjoy.

Talking

If you cannot help but overhear a conversation, there may be a message in it that you are meant to hear.

CHAPTER 23

MISCELLANEOUS SIGNS

Some of the signs that you encounter during the casting of the Living Oracle do not fit into the sign categories of previous chapters. Miscellaneous signs may be less common than the other things and activities that you encounter. For this reason, you may want to pay particular attention to them. It is also likely that you will encounter something that is not listed in this glossary. When this happens use your intuition and interpret through symbolic association.

ARCHES

Arches symbolize the universal law: *There is always another way*. They are a message of openings, opportunities, and movement from one phase of life to another. Small or large, arches over a small garden or over a bridge are a sign that you are moving into a new cycle of life.

BABY STROLLER

Encountering a baby carriage or stroller is a sign of rebirth, the return to innocence and new beginnings. It can also signify a new situation or positive development. If you want to have a child, this is an auspicious sign of a coming pregnancy.

BALLOONS

Encountering balloons is a message to enjoy and celebrate the small things in life with a childlike sense of wonder. They may also be telling you to shed your worries and stress and rise above the troubling and mundane ups and downs of life. Happiness and good news are coming your way.

BILLBOARD

Given their size you are likely to notice a billboard. It may or may not have a message for you. If you encounter one, pause, read it, and feel for any connection you have to its images and message. You will know by the feelings it illicits in you if there is a personal message. Look for words that may have dual or personal meaning.

BELL TOWER

A bell tower is a sign of recognition and praise from the spirit realm. Your recent actions and positive intent are seen and appreciated. If the bell is ringing, your accomplishments and efforts will be seen and recognized by others. It may also be a sign to become more involved with the community and to share your gifts with others.

BIRD NEST

A bird nest is a sign of the love and care that the divine has for you. It can also be a message of relationship harmony, a new home, or home renovation, and it can be a suggestion to settle into your current situation. You are where you are meant to be.

BODY DOUBLE

If you encounter someone who looks and reminds you of a loved one who has passed over, this may be a sign that they are close and guiding you. This may be a message that your loved one is influencing the other signs and messages that you receive while you are casting the oracle.

BOTANICAL GARDEN

A botanical garden is a sign of contentment, peace, and rejuvenation. It is a message to trust that a higher power is working out a current issue or condition.

BRIDGE

Bridges symbolize a crucial time of transition from one state to another. This may be leaving behind a relationship, job, a state of mind, or an aspect of who and what you have thought yourself to be. A bridge is a message to leave the past behind and venture into new possibilities, ideas, and adopt a new attitude and perspective.

BUMPER STICKERS

Bumper stickers may have a personal message for you. Pay attention to any of them that you notice. Look for puns, double meanings, or synchronicities.

CAR REPAIR SHOP

A car repair shop is a sign to seek guidance, advice, or insight from another, possibly a professional. This may be a message to fine-tune your skills and abilities and be at your optimum state—mind, body, and spirit. This may also be a message to get a health checkup.

CAR WASH

Symbolic of revitalization, a car wash is a sign that you may be absorbing negative energy and allowing others to affect your moods and sense of well-being. Become aware of the people and situations that create stress and tension, and protect yourself from their influence. A car wash may also be a message to detox the physical body, purge negative thoughts, and forgive yourself and others.

CARNIVAL

If you encounter a carnival, street fair, or party, it is a message that you may need to get out of your routines, try something new, and explore your creativity. It is also a suggestion to lighten up and not take life too seriously.

If you encounter clowns, mimes, or street theater, it is a sign that you are not seeing the events and people in your life with clarity. Others may not be showing you their true selves, or you may be being fooled or tricked.

CAST

Encountering someone with a cast on their leg or arm or in a brace is a sign of protection, healing, recovery, and limitation. At times limitations are a way of protecting us from making mistakes and creating difficulties. Although we all want to receive what we want when we want it, this is a message to be patient and know that there is an inner process of healing taking place that is strengthening you.

CELL PHONE TOWER

A cell phone tower is a sign of communication of a large scale. It may be that the spirit realm is broadcasting a message to you or that you have the ability to communicate with higher spiritual energies. It may also be a sign of your influence with others and that you have a message to share.

CEMETERY/GRAVEYARD

Encountering a graveyard is a message of transition and change. It may indicate that an idea, possibility, desire, or wish has been laid to rest. It often signifies rest and recuperation before going forward with change. It may be a sign of letting someone or something go and not looking into the past. In rare cases, it is a message that someone is ill and may be passing over.

COINS

Coins are often a signature sign from a loved one on the other side. Pay attention to the denomination of the coin, as a loved one may send a specific coin—for instance a dime, penny, or quarter—over and over to let you know they are close.

Coins and bills may also be a sign of coming abundance, a message that you are in sync with your soul energy, or a symbol to open your heart to divine blessings.

CHURCH

A church, spiritual center, synagogue, or temple is a symbol of divinity and a sign from your angels, letting you know that they are with you.

You are being watched over and you are loved. A church can represent the need to further explore the divinity within you and to avoid dogma and spiritual prejudice. Open to all beliefs and all people.

If there is a service going on in the church or if the church doors are open, it may be a message for you to share your spirituality with others. If you are more of a loner when it comes to your spiritual beliefs, it is time to share and express this part of yourself with others.

CLOCK

A clock is a sign of time and timing. It may be a message that now is the time to begin or complete a project, relationship, career, or other activity. It might also be a suggestion to be patient while conditions are being worked out for your highest good.

If the clock is not working or not working correctly, it can be a message of an abrupt ending or that someone has passed over to the other side.

CLOTHESLINE

A clothesline with laundry hanging from it is a sign of clearing the mind and emotions of any negative, judgmental, and stressful thoughts and feelings. Focusing on what may appear to be small and insignificant personality deficits and weaknesses and releasing them will allow the light of your soul to shine through. A clothesline may also be a message to be honest and open and allow others to see the true you.

CONSTRUCTION SITE

Encountering a construction site is a sign of the need for active effort. This is not a time to drift or be indecisive but to take action. A construction site could signify building a new career, following through on an opportunity, putting effort into a relationship, or setting your finances in order.

DOGHOUSE

A doghouse is a sign that you may be keeping love and companionship or your emotional feelings at bay. If you are feeling lonely or unable to make meaningful connections with others, reach out in friendship. A doghouse may also be a message that you are feeling guilt or remorse over something you said or did. If this is the case, make amends as best you can, forgive yourself, and move on.

ELECTRICAL TOWER

An electrical tower is a sign of power and stability and can also indicate healing abilities. It may be a message that success will come as you let go of control and join forces with others to mutually support one another's ideas and goals.

ELECTRONICS

The Living Oracle is primarily focused on signs and symbols in the outer world. However, there are a few common signs that you may encounter in your home or office. The spirit realm often sends us signs through electrical-powered devices.

Computers

A computer system problem or crash is a message that you may need to examine your thoughts and change your current thinking. A new approach and perspective is needed

A computer virus may indicate the need to root out negative thoughts. They may be more destructive than you may think. It might also be a sign to be careful with your diet. Avoid food and drink that may be toxic to your system.

Emails

E-mails represent what we are energetically sending out into the world. Problems with e-mailing may be a message to become more aware of what you are broadcasting to others and the energy that you are receiving and taking on.

Persistent junk e-mail or your account being hacked is a message that you are vulnerable to the energy of others, especially toxic emotions and thoughts. You may need to activate a shield or psychic protection around yourself.

Phones

A phone turning off or on by itself is a sign that someone in the spirit realm is attempting to get a message to you. Stop and listen and pay attention to other signs that provide more insight.

A phone that calls others on its own or acts strangely may be a message that you are misinterpreting what another has said or not communicating with others clearly. It might also be a message to contact the person who was "mistakenly" called.

FALLEN ELECTRICAL WIRES

Encountering fallen electrical power lines is a sign of a loss of personal power and a warning to be mindful of the balance of power between yourself and another. You may find yourself on the receiving end of a situation or person who uses their power as force and control. Also be conscious that you are using your power with others fairly and respectfully. Fallen electrical lines can also indicate a health issue.

FEATHERS

Feathers are the calling card of the spirit realm. They may be sent from a spirit guide, a loved one on the other side, an angel, or an earth spirit guardian. The type of feather will give you more information about its meanings. (See *Birds* in the glossary.) Feathers may also be a sign to listen to your intuition and focus on your spirituality and relationship with the divine. You are being guided; trust where you feel led.

FENCE

A fence is a sign of organization, setting limits, and control. It may be that you need to pull in the reins and control yourself or a situation or condition. Alternatively, it may be a message to move out of any self-imposed restrictions or limitations and control of others. A fence may also be a message to avoid gossip and interfering in another's decisions and choices and expect others to respect your privacy.

Barbed Wire
A barbed wire fence may be a warning that someone or something is trying to control you with their words or actions.

White Picket
A white picket fence is an auspicious sign of safety, security, and fulfilling relationships.

FIRE HYDRANT

A fire hydrant with water streaming out of it is a sign that you may be in need of spiritual or emotional support and renewal. This is a message that there are material and spiritual resources available that you can take advantage of.

This might also be a sign that you have an abundance of love and spiritual energy to give to others. It may be a message to give freely to those in need.

FLAG

A flag is a sign of commitment, identity, and the expression of your true self. A flag waving in the breeze may be a message to trust and express your opinions, insights, and ideas, and share them with others. It might also be a sign to pay attention and take action on your intuition, hunches, and gut feelings.

A flag hanging flat against a pole is a sign to align your will to a greater cause or let go of your personal biases and listen to what others around you have to say.

An empty flagpole can be a message to look within and focus on your personal truth. You may be compromising your authentic self in order to fit in with a group or placate others.

FARM

A farm may be a sign that you are working and have big plans, ideas, and aspirations. If the farm is well run and busy, it is a positive sign of abundance and success. If the farm is abandoned or no longer functioning, it is sign that you may need to be careful that you are not being overly idealistic. You may need to get to work on more practical areas. A nonfunctioning farm can also be a warning of loss, especially financial loss. A farm may also indicate your innate ability to nurture and care for others.

FLEA MARKET, YARD SALE

A flea market or yard sale is a sign to build on what you have before starting a new project, changing careers, leaving a job, or making a change in investments. Abundance will come as you review what you have already attained and capitalize on what is working. It may also be a sign that you are living in the past. Learn the lessons of past experiences and move on.

FOUND OBJECTS

Encountering small, found objects is a sign that you will soon be in the company of interesting people or have the opportunity to engage in out-of-your-normal-routine activities. Also pay attention to what you find, as the message might be in the object itself.

Credit Card

Finding a credit card is a sign to be honest and act with integrity. It may be a message to improve, heal, and increase your sense of self-worth. Embrace and perceive your true value.

Earring

Finding an earring may be a message to listen within or to those around you better. You may not be truly hearing what another or a spirit being is saying.

Child's Toy

A child's toy is a sign to allow your inner child to emerge or to take some time for yourself and relax and play.

Glasses

Finding glasses or sunglasses is a sign that you are not seeing or perceiving a situation, yourself, or another with clarity. There may be something or someone in your life that you are taking for granted.

Purse or Wallet

Finding another's purse or wallet is a sign that you are relying on others' opinions or judgments more than your own. This is a message to own your power and be more self-reliant.

Ring

Finding a ring is a message to give more of yourself to another or to put effort into a project that benefits others. You have been given gifts that you need to share. This is a message from the higher realms of love and wisdom to extend yourself and give to those in need.

Watch

Finding a watch is a sign that it is time to take action on a project, dream, or idea. If you are procrastinating, this is message to move forward. If you have been busy and overwhelmed this is a sign to slow down and allow others to help you.

FUNERAL PROCESSION

You are in the midst of a transformation. More change is on the way. Slow down and become aware of what you most want and desire. Allow for new perspectives and possibilities. Be patient, new beginnings and inspiration are on the way.

GARBAGE

Garbage is a clear message that you need to let go of what is no longer serving you. This might be anger, painful wounds, negativity, limited thoughts and beliefs, or it might be a relationship or situation. Become aware of any negativity that you may have absorbed from others. This might also indicate the need to detox and cleanse the physical body.

GLASS WINDOWS

Large glass windows can be a sign to open your mind to new perceptions. There may be something you are missing or not correctly perceiving. It can also be a sign of the need to see the big picture and to take a hard look at what is going on in your life.

Broken

Broken glass can be a sign of hurt feelings, criticism, and the need to be cautious in your dealings with others.

A cracked or shattered storefront or home window is a message that your perception of your present situation may be skewed or illusionary.

GREENHOUSE

A greenhouse can be a message to focus on your growth and to cultivate new ideas and creativity. It can signal the need to take better care of yourself or that something or someone in your life needs special attention.

HAMMOCK

An empty hammock is a sign of rest and relaxation. You are being given the message to commune with nature, daydream, and take a break.

Encountering someone in a hammock is a message that there may be someone in your life who is taking advantage of you, is not fully present, or is not taking on equal responsibility.

HUBCAP

A positive omen that higher forces are aligned in your favor. Symbolic of a pentagon, hubcaps symbolize your connection to the earth, the natural elements, and spirit.

JET TRAIL

Seeing a jet trail, but no jet, is a sign from the spirit realm that they see and know your actions, thoughts, and feelings. Higher forces are guiding and leading you.

JUNK

Encountering junk or a junkyard is a message to revisit the past or something that you have walked away from or left behind. There is a valuable lesson, insight, or creative possibility that you need to claim. This could be a message to revisit an old relationship.

KITE

A kite is symbolic of your hopes, aspirations, and dreams. If the kite is on the ground or damaged, it indicates that you need to focus on finding the best circumstances and opportunities for launching your dreams. It is time to be grounded and practical.

A kite flying in a blue, clear sky indicates the attainment of your hopes and desires. It is time to spread your positivity and shine.

A kite flying in cloudy skies is a message of coming success and achieving your goals and dreams. Your efforts are going to be realized, despite appearances to the contrary.

A kite flying over the water is symbolic of spiritual and emotional well-being and enlightenment. It is a message of oneness and connection with the spirit realm.

LADDERS

Encountering a ladder is a message to elevate your thoughts to a higher perspective. Your thinking is limited. Open to possibilities and try to see the big picture.

LOST DOG OR CAT SIGN

Encountering a sign for a lost dog or cat can be a message for you to not allow a difficult situation or person to rob you of your self-esteem, joy, and positive feelings of love.

MIRROR

A mirror may be a message imploring you take a look at yourself and be sure that your life is reflecting your innermost self and what is true and important for you.

A cracked or shattered mirror may be a message to break negative habits and routines. It can also be a sign of upcoming disappointment and betrayal.

NUCLEAR POWER PLANT

A nuclear power plant symbolizes a condition, relationship, or issue that may require more from you than you are able to give. With great potential comes great risk. This is a message to carefully consider your options and weigh your available resources, time, and energy before going forward.

ORBS

Seeing orbs or streams or flashes of light or color is a sign that a loved on the other side, an angel, or spirit guide is present and guiding you. This is an auspicious sign of love, spiritual presence, and fulfillment.

PARADE

Encountering a parade, even if it is just a small group, is a message of honor and celebration. You have recently or you are presently experiencing an opportunity to walk away from old and outworn thoughts, beliefs, and behaviors and enter into a higher perspective and acceptance of self. The parade is cheering you on.

PARASAILING

Seeing someone parasailing is symbolic of freeing yourself and allowing your spirit to guide you. It can indicate that your dreams, efforts, and goals are being supported by the spiritual realm. Your path is being prepared before you. Relax and enjoy the journey.

PARK

A park is a message to take it easy, contemplate the simple beauty of life, and refresh your spirit. A park may also be a sign of a romantic relationship coming your way or being rekindled.

PARKING METERS

Parking meters are a sign to be careful not to waste time and resources on desires and activities that will ultimately not be in your best interest. Even small mistakes and indulgences can be costly.

PLAYGROUND

A playground for children symbolizes the inner child's need to play and escape the daily stresses of adult responsibilities. See through the eyes of your inner child and the world is filled with wonder and magic. A playground can also foretell a pregnancy.

PAVILION

A pavilion is a sign of an open mind, sharing ideas, joining with others, and gaining influence. You are going through a transformation and new dreams, relationships, and goals are beginning to take root and manifest.

A pavilion full of people is a sign of coming success and a message to continue going forward with new ideas, projects, and relationships.

SAFETY CONES

Orange safety cones symbolize the need for you to be cautious, alert, and pay attention to details. They are a message to focus on what may appear to be minor and small issues. In this way you are able to circumvent challenges and difficulties.

SPORTS FIELD

Encountering a baseball, football, soccer, or other professional sports recreational field is symbolic of the game of life, especially in relation to confronting upcoming challenges. They are a sign of competitiveness, the need to excel and come out on top. Playing fields also indicate enjoyment and playing the game of life with gusto.

STATUE, SCULPTURE

Statues are a reminder from the spirit realm that there is a positive part or aspect of yourself that is dormant and needs to come to life.

A statue of an angel, fairy, saint, or other divine being is a sign that this being is with you and guiding you. Take a moment to listen to the message that this divine presence has for you.

A statue honoring a person from the past is a sign to become aware of and embrace your courage, determination, and the purpose that you have come here to express and share. Live life now.

An artistic or abstract sculpture is a sign to let others and the world see the true you. It is a message from the spirit realm reminding you to know that you are a unique, individualized expression of the divine; a perfect being. Express your authentic self.

STORAGE UNIT

A moveable self-storage unit that you encounter in a driveway or on the side of the road is a sign of slow change and possible procrastination. It also signifies effort in organizing and planning for the future. You may want to consider if there is something that you need to let go of in order to move forward.

A storage unit building has a bit of a different message. Encountering a building of storage units is a message that you are clinging to the past and old, outworn memories, beliefs, ideas, emotional energy, and judgments. It is costing you. It is time to look within and release what no longer serves you.

TENT

A tent is a message from the spirit realm that wherever you are, you are being watched over and protected. It may be a message to seek spiritual shelter from emotional or other difficulties. Whatever you are currently experiencing is only temporary.

A large event tent is a sign to seek out and join with others of like mind for a common goal or experience. It may also be a message to network and make the most out your current connections.

An empty event tent is a message to let go and move on from a situation or relationship. The connection was not meant to be long-term.

TIRES

Encountering new tires that are not on a car can be a motivating sign encouraging you to take action and get going on a project, relationship, or goal. It is a sign of progress and swift attainment.

Old tires, or tires that are not on a car, can be a sign of weariness, exhaustion, and a message to change the path that you are on.

TREEHOUSE

A treehouse is a sign that you may need some time and space away from everyday stress, responsibilities, and worries. Inspiration comes from childlike openness and adventure. Use your imagination and transport yourself from the routine and mundane into the open field of possibilities.

UMBRELLA

An umbrella is a sign of resources, shelter, and protection. If the umbrella is being used during rain, it may be a sign that you possess the inner power to take care of yourself and may indicate the need for self-protection. The focus is on you. A small handheld umbrella can be a sign of solitude and the need to trust yourself and your intuition. If the umbrella is closed or not in use, it can be a sign to be alert to present or upcoming issues with others and to be mindful of your self-interests.

A larger porch or deck umbrella can be a sign of receiving or offering shelter, protection, and help to others. If someone or something needs help and assistance, this is a sign to lend a hand. Alternatively, if you are needing help or advice, ask for it and be willing to let others be there for you.

VACANT LOT

A vacant lot is a sign of hidden potential and a message to be creative and open to possibilities. Act with intent and purpose. It can also be a message to let go of your judgments and perceive the goodness and worthiness within yourself, your situation, or within another.

WINDMILL

A sign of increased mental energy, a windmill can indicate that divine guidance is coming through your thoughts. Alternatively it may be a sign of scattered thinking and the need to focus and organize your ideas and thoughts and come up with a plan. If you have been feeling scattered and unsure of what direction to take or have a pending decision, a windmill is a sign to put your thoughts into action.

ZOO

A zoo is a sign that you may be keeping your more primal instincts and emotions, or interesting and unique qualities and characteristics, locked away. Instead of trying to fit in and being who and what others expect you to be, be yourself. Find others who share your interests and preferences and express all of you.

BIBLIOGRAPHY AND RECOMMENDED READING

Andrews, Ted. *Animal-Speak: The Spiritual & Magical Powers of Creatures Great & Small.* St. Paul, MN: Llewellyn Worldwide, 2002.

———. *How to Meet and Work with Spirit Guides.* St. Paul, MN: Llewellyn Worldwide, 2002.

Blavatsky, H. P. *Collected Writings, Vol. III.* Wheaton, IL: Theosophical Publishing House, 1968.

Blum, Ralph. *The Book of Runes: A Handbook for the Use of an Ancient Oracle.* New York, NY: St. Martins Press, 1987.

Bollingen Series. *The I Ching, or, Book of Changes (Bollingen Series XIX).* Princeton, NJ: Princeton University Press; 3rd edition, 1967.

Calabrese, Adrian. *Sacred Signs: Hear, See & Believe. Messages from the Universe.* Woodbury, MN: Llewellyn Worldwide, 2006.

Castaneda, Carlos. *The Fire From Within.* New York, NY: Simon and Shuster, 1984.

Choquette, Sonia. *Ask Your Guides: Connecting to Your Divine Support System.* Carlsbad, CA: Hay House, 2006.

Crisp, Tony. *Dream Dictionary: The A to Z Guide to Understanding Your Unconscious Mind.* New York, NY: Dell Publishing, 2002.

Geer, Mary K. *Greer's 21 Ways to Read a Tarot Card.* Woodbury, MN: Llewellyn Worldwide, 2006.

Gong, Rosemary. *Good Luck Life: The Essential Guide to Chinese American Celebrations and Culture.* New York, NY: William Morrow Paperbacks, 2005.

Grasse, Ray. *The Waking Dream: Unlocking the Symbolic Language of Our Lives.* Wheaton, IL: Quest Books, 1996.

Holloway, Gillian. *The Complete Dream Book: Discover What Your Dreams Reveal about You and Your Life.* Chicago, IL: Source Books, 2006.

Jung, Carl Gustav, ed. *Man and His Symbols.* Garden City, NY: Doubleday, 1964.

Lake-Thorn, Robert. *Spirits of the Earth: A Guide to Native American Nature Symbols, Stories, and Ceremonies.* New York, NY: Plume Publishing, 1997.

Louis, Anthony. *Tarot Plain and Simple.* St. Paul, MN: Llewellyn Publications, 2002.

Moore, Barbara. *Tarot Spreads: Layouts & Techniques to Empower Your Readings.* Woodbury, MN: Llewellyn Worldwide, 2010.

Peschel, Lisa. *A Practical Guide to the Runes: Their Uses in Divination and Magic.* St. Paul, MN: Llewellyn Worldwide, 1989.

Riske, Kris Brandt. *Llewellyn's Complete Book of Astrology: The Easy Way to Learn Astrology.* Woodbury, MN: Llewellyn Worldwide, 2007.

Smith, Ramsey, W. *Myths and Legends of the Australian Aborigines.* Mineola, NY: Dover Publications, 2003.

Tedeschi, Kevin J. *The Encyclopedia of Symbolism.* New York, NY: Berkley Publishing Group, 1995.

Virtue, Doreen. *Signs From Above: Your Angels' Messages about Your Life Purpose, Relationships, Health, and More.* Carlsbad, CA: Hay House Publishing, 2006.

———. *Angel Numbers 101: The Meaning of 111, 123, 444, and Other Number Sequences.* Carlsbad, CA: Hay House Publishing, 2008.

INDEX

To Write to the Author

If you wish to contact the author or would like more information about this book, please write to the author in care of Llewellyn Worldwide Ltd. and we will forward your request. Both the author and publisher appreciate hearing from you and learning of your enjoyment of this book and how it has helped you. Llewellyn Worldwide Ltd. cannot guarantee that every letter written to the author can be answered, but all will be forwarded. Please write to:

Sherrie Dillard
℅ Llewellyn Worldwide
2143 Wooddale Drive
Woodbury, MN 55125-2989

Please enclose a self-addressed stamped envelope for reply,
or $1.00 to cover costs. If outside the U.S.A., enclose
an international postal reply coupon.

Many of Llewellyn's authors have websites with additional information and resources. For more information, please visit our website at http://www.llewellyn.com